# Vocabulary Virtuoso

## PSAT-SAT Book 1

Vocabulary Virtuoso products available in print or eBook form.

Primary • Elementary • Middle School
PSAT-SAT Book 1 • PSAT-SAT Book 2

Written by
**Nancy Forderer**

Cover Design by
**Kseniya Belysheva**

Edited by
**Patricia Gray**

THE CRITICAL THINKING CO.™
www.CriticalThinking.com
Phone: 800-458-4849 • Fax: 541-756-1758
1991 Sherman Ave., Suite 200 • North Bend • OR 97459
ISBN 978-1-60144-936-8

Printed in the United States of America by McNaughton & Gunn, Inc., Saline, MI (Apr. 2018)

# Table of Contents

## About the Author

Nancy Forderer is a retired educator who taught language arts to middle school and high school students for 25 years. She received her B.Ed. and M.E. in secondary education from the University of Toledo in Toledo, Ohio. Currently, Ms. Forderer resides in San Diego, California, near her family. She enjoys tutoring, writing, reading, and traveling.

# Introduction

William Funk, author, poet, and lexicographer once said, "The more words you know, the more clearly and powerfully you will think...and the more ideas you will invite into your mind."

The verbal section of the new SAT test has critical reading sections that closely resemble the type of reading the student will encounter in college and in future work situations. Both the writing and language sections in the new SAT test the student's ability to analyze and think clearly, and as William Funk states, comprehension in reading, as well as cogent thinking skills, are strengthened by a strong vocabulary.

*Vocabulary Virtuoso: PSAT-SAT* was created for late middle school and high school students to build vocabulary necessary for comprehension in critical reading.

Nine words are in each of the twenty lessons and 85% of all words are from current PSAT or SAT lists. Additional words have a link to academic curriculum content.

Each vocabulary list emphasizes one part of speech such as nouns, verbs, or adjectives. The lessons include a pronunciation key, definition, other word forms, and a sentence using the word in context.

After each lesson, varied creative activities follow, in which the student uses the words in context. The story in each lesson follows a literary thread using concepts from academic content in language arts, literature, and the humanities.

As in previous *Vocabulary Virtuoso* books, the action in the stories takes place in a fictional classroom setting where students and teachers interact as they learn the following concepts:

**Literary**

Characterization in Literature

| | |
|---|---|
| Idioms | Euphemisms |
| Puns | Aphorisms |
| Jargon | Allusions |
| Irony | Theme |

**Rhetorical**

The Art of Persuasion in Speech and Writing
Using the Extended Simile to Write a Poem

**Historical**

The Renaissance
Renaissance Artists

A review lesson is included after every four lessons to ensure mastery of the words. The review lesson includes three activities, one of which is a crossword puzzle.

# Vocabulary List 1
## Amazing Adjectives

**Word**
[pronunciation]
**other word form**

**Definition**
• sample sentence

| Word | Definition |
|---|---|
| **effervescent**<br>[ef er VES uhnt]<br>**effervescence** (n) | lively, high-spirited, enthusiastic<br>• Emmalin has an effervescent personality. |
| **mawkish**<br>[MAW kish] | excessively sentimental, often in a silly way<br>• Barbara became mawkish when she saw the movie *Lion King*. |
| **parsimonious**<br>[pahr suh MOH nee uhs]<br>**parsimony** (n) | frugal to the point of stinginess<br>• The parsimonious woman only spent money for basic necessities. |
| **perspicacious**<br>[pur spi KEY shuhs] | having mental perception and understanding<br>• His perspicacious financial advisor warned him that the stock market would decline. |
| **spurious**<br>[SPUR ee uhs] | not genuine, authentic, true, or sincere<br>• The facts proved that his claim of being an Austrian prince was spurious. |
| **surreptitious**<br>[suhr ep TISH uhs] | marked by stealth and secrecy<br>• She was surreptitious and hid her sister's gift under blankets in the closet. |
| **tantamount**<br>[TAN tuh mount] | equal in value, meaning, or effect<br>• Ms. Cosgrove reminded her students that always eating junk food is tantamount to deliberately destroying your health. |
| **truculent**<br>[TRUHK yu luhnt]<br>**truculence** (n) | easily annoyed and always ready to argue or fight<br>• The boss became truculent whenever anyone challenged his authority. |
| **visceral**<br>[VIS er uhl] | instinctive feelings not based on reason or logic<br>• Celeste has a visceral fear of being in crowded places. |

**A.** Write the best list word that the synonyms, idioms, or phrases define to complete each sentence.

| | | | |
|---|---|---|---|
| mawkish | spurious | surreptitious | frugal |
| parsimonious | effervescent | tantamount | truculent |
| visceral | perspicacious | | |

1. Her fear of mice is ______________________ and every time she sees one, she feels like she might faint.

   intuitive deep-down ingrained innate

2. The FBI ran a/an ______________________ operation to infiltrate hate groups in the U.S.A.

   clandestine on the sly covert furtive

3. On New Years Eve, the crowd in Times Square in New York City is a/an ______________________ group of revelers.

   vivacious sparkling bubbly ebullient

4. Luke's mom was much too ______________________ to believe his flimsy excuse for coming home late.

   discerning shrewd insightful astute

5. The Van Gogh painting was proven to be a/an ______________________ reproduction.

   bogus fraudulent phony counterfeit

6. Tim's dad was ______________________ about giving his children money and insisted that they work for their allowances.

   penny-pinching Scrooge-like greedy miserly

7. "Getting an A from Ms. Palmer on a speech is ______________________ to winning the lottery," noted Rachel.

   comparable on a par with as good as commensurate

8. "Grandma is always ______________________ when she sees us," laughed Piper. "Cheek-pinching, a few tears, and icky-lipstick kisses are always part of her greeting."

   maudlin mushy cloying sappy

9. The ______________________ comments exchanged by the men led to a fist fight.

   antagonistic combative pugnacious belligerent

 

**B.** Write the best word from the choice box to complete each sentence.

| | | | |
|---|---|---|---|
| truculence | parsimony | tantamount | surreptitious |
| perspicacious | mawkish | visceral | infallible |
| effervescence | spurious | | |

1. Suzanne's ______________________ is obvious when she refuses to lend her classmates lunch money or school supplies.

2. "We need to be ______________________ when we plan Rachel's surprise birthday party," warned Piper. "If she sees us whispering together, she may get suspicious."

3. "Revealing my secret would be ______________________ to deliberately destroying our friendship," warned Max.

4. "Is this another ______________________ excuse?" queried Ms. Patterson when Ned said he mistakenly thought his essay wasn't due until next week.

5. Emmalin's ______________________ brightens up a room when she enters.

6. "I have a/an ______________________ hatred for those who abuse animals," declared Caroline.

7. Her classmates often consult Ann when they have a problem, because she is a good listener and a/an ______________________ person.

8. "Cindy, crying about your bad hair day is a bit ______________________. Stop or everyone will laugh at you," warned Heidi.

9. Luke's ______________________ toward his classmates is the reason why he has few friends.

**C. Story Challenge**
Write the best word from the choice box to fill each blank in the story.

| | | | |
|---|---|---|---|
| tantamount | effervescent | mawkish | parsimonious |
| peripatetic | truculent | visceral | perspicacious |
| surreptitious | spurious | | |

## Showing and Not Telling

"Fiction writers try to create believable characters," Mr. Riley stated in writing class. "As readers, sometimes we have a/an (1)____________________ reaction to a believable character, not a reaction based on reason or logic. For example, in Shakespeare's *Romeo and Juliet*, the reader might instinctively cheer for the young lovers to be together, without considering the negative consequences of Romeo and Juliet's forbidden love. This reaction is not (2)____________________ or overly sentimental, but is sincere because through the characters' actions and words, Shakespeare created Romeo and Juliet as young lovers who yearn to be together."

Mr. Riley continued, "Today, we'll explore ways in which authors create believable literary characters. First, good fiction writers 'show, not tell.' Can you give examples of what this means using the books and plays you've read in literature classes?"

Hillary raised her hand to respond. "In the book *To Kill a Mockingbird*, Atticus Finch is a/an (3)____________________ father—one who is attentive to his children, who explains life situations to them, and who insists that they respect others," offered Hillary. "Author Harper Lee doesn't tell us that Atticus is an excellent parent, but the reader understands that his actions and words are (4)____________________ to those of a good, caring parent," Hillary said.

Bernie was eager to share an example. "I have another example from *Romeo and Juliet*," he said. "Shakespeare doesn't tell us that the character Tybalt is (5)____________________, but by Tybalt's words and actions and the way the other characters react to him, the reader sees that Tybalt is hot-headed and always trying to start a fight. For example, Mercutio, who hates Tybalt, gives him the nickname "The Prince of Cats," because Tybalt always seems to be looking for a fight."

"Excellent example, Bernie. In another of Shakespeare's plays, *Julius Caesar*," added Mr. Riley, "the behavior of Brutus is (6)____________________. Brutus pretends to be Caesar's friend, but is being (7)____________________ because he is involved in a plot to murder him. Shakespeare uses the words, thoughts, and actions of Brutus to show, not tell what he is planning, and also to show how Brutus is conflicted about what he is about to do."

Mr. Riley continued, "Another good example of a character revealed by words is also from the play *Julius Caesar*: Cassius says, "Caesar…no mightier than you or I, yet prodigious grown…" Can anyone explain what Cassius' words mean, and what his words tell us about the character, Cassius?"

Suzanne explained, "Cassius is plotting against Caesar and from his words, the reader knows Cassius is trying to convince the others that Caesar is becoming too powerful. Cassius is saying that even though Caesar is no better than all of us, he has become much more powerful."

"Excellent analysis, Suzanne." Mr. Riley continued, "Besides showing the character in action, the author often lets the reader see a character's thoughts. During Shakespeare's time, the audience would often know a character's thoughts through an "aside"—a remark made by a character intended to be heard by the audience but not heard by the other characters in the play."

"You may recall when you were younger, reading the book *Lunch Money* by Andrew Clements," reminded Mr. Riley, "the character Greg is obsessive about making and saving money. The author uses third-person-limited point of view, so the reader knows by Greg's thoughts, as well as by his words and actions, that he is (8)_________________________ without the author Andrew Clements telling us."

Elsie had an answer. "When Ebenezer Scrooge discovers the real meaning of Christmas in *A Christmas Carol*, he is laughing and crying and at the same time saying, "I am light as a feather, I am happy as an angel, I am as merry as a schoolboy…" Through the character's words and actions, Charles Dickens shows the reader that Scrooge is (9)_________________________."

"Excellent work today, class. When you write your own character analyses, remember to explain how authors reveal character."

Create Characters – Show, Not Tell

- Character description, words, actions, and thoughts
- Reactions by others to the character
- Words to or about the character by others

**D.** The underlined part in each sentence is a synonym, idiom, phrase, or definition for a list word. Unscramble the list word and write the word on the blank.

1. An <u>instinctive</u> fear overwhelms me whenever I'm standing in line to ride a roller coaster, " said Hope. ________________ clsevair

2. Luke becomes extremely <u>argumentative</u> whenever someone criticizes him. ________________ lutenurtc

3. A <u>high-spirited</u> mood prevailed in the classroom when Ms. Paterson postponed the grammar test for a week. ________________ evfenrctsefe

4. Kara becomes <u>tearful</u> when she reminisces about her childhood in Vancouver, Canada. ________________ khwimas

5. "Facts must be verified in order to avoid <u>fraudulent</u> information in persuasive writing," said Ms. Paterson. ________________ ursopsui

6. Julia wrote a very <u>perceptive</u> analysis of the novel *Wonder* by R.J. Palacio. ________________ saopieuspricc

7. Mandy was <u>stealthy</u> when she hid her diary under the mattress in her bedroom. ________________ ssuurtreptiio

8. Ned claimed that his track team winning the state championship was <u>equal</u> to winning an Olympic gold medal. ________________ mtotannatu

9. Celeste was <u>miserly</u> with her allowance because she was saving money to buy a new smart phone. ________________ usonaisoprmi

**E.** Write the word, idiom, or phrase from the choice box that best defines each list word.

- sneaky
- maudlin
- bad-tempered
- ingrained
- grandiose
- fake
- penny-pinching
- bubbly
- equal to
- insightful

1. parsimonious ____________________

2. effervescent ____________________

3. perspicacious ____________________

4. spurious ____________________

5. surreptitious ____________________

6. truculent ____________________

7. visceral ____________________

8. mawkish ____________________

9. tantamount ____________________

**F.** Complete each sentence to show that you understand the meaning of the underlined word.

1. Heidi gave her friend a note in a surreptitious way by ______________________________

______________________________________________________________________.

2. Luke displayed truculent behavior when he ______________________________

______________________________________________________________________.

3. The spurious claim that Cindy gave for not having her homework was that ____________

______________________________________________________________________.

4. "Going to the dentist to have a tooth pulled is tantamount to ______________________

__________________________________________________," said Ned.

5. Suzanne is so parsimonious that she ______________________________

______________________________________________________________________.

6. Every time Rachel hears ______________________________ she becomes mawkish and starts to ______________________________.

7. Casey had a visceral reaction when he discovered that ______________________________

______________________________________________________________________.

8. Emmalin, an effervescent person, greets her friends by ______________________________

______________________________________________________________________.

9. Christopher's grandfather gave perspicacious advice to his grandchildren by telling them

______________________________________________________________________.

# Vocabulary List 2
## Admirable Adverbs

| **Word**<br>[pronunciation]<br>**other word form**<br> | **Definition**<br>• sample sentence<br> |
|---|---|
| **impertinently**<br>[im PUR tuh nent lee]<br>**impertinence** (n) | not showing proper respect<br>• In class, he impertinently put his feet on his desk and refused to remove his sunglasses. |
| **inconspicuously**<br>[in kuhn SPIK yoo uhs lee] | not noticeable or prominent<br>• Inconspicuously, Heidi entered the auditorium and sat in a seat in the back. |
| **ingeniously**<br>[in JEEN yuhs lee]<br>**ingenuity** (n) | creatively or imaginatively<br>• Inventor, Albert J. Parkhouse ingeniously created the first clothes hanger. |
| **inquisitively**<br>[in KWIZ ih tiv lee] | given to inquiry, research, or asking questions<br>• The little girl inquisitively asked how clouds were made. |
| **judiciously**<br>[joo DISH uhs lee] | in a way that shows good judgment<br>• Max judiciously decided to do his most difficult assignment first. |
| **obnoxiously**<br>[uhb NOK shuhs lee] | highly objectionable or offensively<br>• Mom made him apologize when he obnoxiously burped at the table. |
| **reluctantly**<br>[ree LUHK tuhnt lee]<br>**reluctance** (n) | feeling or showing hesitation, aversion, or unwillingness<br>• Kara reluctantly took a bite of the eggplant casserole. |
| **solemnly**<br>[SOL uhm lee]<br>**solemnity** (n) | in a dignified and thoughtful way<br>• The mourners solemnly stood near the grave site. |
| **unethically**<br>[uhn ETH ih kuhl lee] | against proper rules of conduct or morality<br>• The businessman was accused of unethically trying to avoid paying taxes. |

**A.** Write the best list word that the synonyms, idioms, or phrases define to complete each sentence.

| | | | |
|---|---|---|---|
| impertinently | judiciously | inquisitively | reluctantly |
| solemnly | ingeniously | obnoxiously | unethically |
| inconspicuously | coherently | | |

1. Piper's young brother Charlie ____________________________ asked where light goes when you turn it off.

   curiously inquiringly probingly speculatively

2. Celeste ____________________________ promised not to reveal Cindy's secret.

   formally earnestly seriously gravely

3. Casey, ____________________________ agreed to be Caroline's partner in a square dance in gym class.

   unwillingly unenthusiastically warily hesitantly

4. Ms. Palmer demonstrated to her students how they can ____________________________ do deep breathing to relieve anxiety before giving a speech.

   hesitantly unobtrusively surreptitiously unnoticeably

5. The president ____________________________ makes a decision after listening to all sides and considering all points of view.

   wisely sensibly prudently astutely

6. The man was able to enter Tim's grandparent's home by ____________________________ pretending to be from the local gas company checking for a gas leak.

   perfidiously unscrupulously dishonestly deceitfully

7. The maître d' at the restaurant tried to appease the customer when he loudly and ____________________________ complained about the service.

   annoyingly unpleasantly repulsively offensively

8. Aiden could ____________________________ solve most math problems in his head.

   skillfully deftly innovatively cleverly

9. Milly's sister is a stand-up comedian and says that hecklers who ____________________________ yell insults from the audience are an annoying part of the job.

   insolently rudely impolitely brazenly

**B.** Write the best word from the choice box to complete each sentence.

| | | | |
|---|---|---|---|
| solemnity | ingenuity | inconspicuously | reluctance |
| impertinence | inquisitively | judiciously | coherently |
| unethically | obnoxiously | | |

1. Everyone clapped for Gary's ______________________ when he made an ace-of-spades change colors and then disappear as he entertained his friends with his repertoire of card tricks.

2. Becky ______________________ entered the classroom and took her seat hoping that Mr. Clark wouldn't notice that she was late.

3. With ______________________, the graduates marched into the auditorium, but after they had all received their diplomas, they cheered and tossed their caps into the air.

4. When the park ranger asked for a volunteer, Mrs. Bradley stepped forward with ______________________ to hold the orange-striped, four-foot corn snake, even though she feared snakes.

5. "Whatever," Luke responded with ______________________, when Ms. Paterson reminded him that failure to turn in his writing folder would have a serious impact on his final grade.

6. Principal Zhang ______________________ invited Hannah and Mandy to use his office to resolve their argument when he noticed them having a noisy altercation in the hallway.

7. Hope explained that her twin brother, Harvey, ______________________ burps at the lunch table just to get attention.

8. In a debate about media censorship, Ned argued that some music lyrics ______________________ use words and ideas that are racist and degrading to women.

9. Her classmates looked ______________________ at Rachel when she entered the classroom on crutches with her left leg in a cast.

## C. Story Challenge

Write the best word from the choice box to fill each blank in the story.

| | | | |
|---|---|---|---|
| inconspicuously | inquisitively | reluctantly | solemnly |
| ingeniously | judiciously | clairvoyantly | unethically |
| impertinently | obnoxiously | | |

### Methods of Characterization

In writing class, Mr. Riley decided to use the vocabulary list of adverbs to continue his lesson on the importance of "showing, not telling" in creating characters when writing fiction. He explained that direct characterization was telling, and the preferred method—indirect characterization was showing.

"Today's task is to invent a setting and a situation and then add a character using one or more indirect methods of characterization. As an extra challenge, use a vocabulary word from this week's list to show how the character is revealed. I'll provide an example to begin," he said

After the students had copied the vocabulary words and definitions into their notebooks, Mr. Riley gave an example.

> The Setting and Situation: Bobby and his mother are in the hall outside the classroom on his first day of kindergarten.
>
> Bobby clung to his mother's leg. "No," he wailed, "I don't want to."

"By Bobby's actions and words, we know how he feels about going to kindergarten," said Mr. Riley. "He is acting (1) ______________________________."

After working silently for fifteen minutes, the students were anxious to give their examples and Matt offered to give the first example.

> The Setting and Situation: Biology class—Andy is sitting across the room from Kim.
>
> "I wonder what I need to do to get her to notice me?" thought Andy as he glanced in Kim's direction.

"(2) ______________________________ is the word," said Becky. "Matt uses Andy's thoughts to show that he likes Kim, and he's curious about what he can do to get her attention."

Becky provided the next example.

The Setting and Situation: Kids are entering a classroom chatting and laughing.

"What's going on with Brandon?" Kyle asked Ben as they watched Brandon silently walk into the room with his head down and slump into the last seat in the third row.

Casey had the answer. "Through Kyle and Ben talking about him and by his actions, we know that Brandon is acting (3) ______________________________, because for some reason he doesn't want anyone to notice him."

"I'll give the next example," said Casey.

The Setting and Situation: The school cafeteria–Blair is sitting at a table with her friends.

"I can't stand how Trevor uses loud burping and weird noises to get attention," said Blair.

"I know," said Justin. "Casey is using what Blair says about Trevor to show how he acts (4) ______________________________," Justin explained.

Hope had her hand up and Mr. Riley called on her to give her example.

The Setting and Situation: Math class and the teacher is passing back tests.

Paul flushed with embarrassment when Mr. Sanders handed back his test and called him lazy and ignorant and said he was wasting his time coming to class. Angrily, Paul threw his test on the floor and left the room slamming the door.

Hannah knew the answer. "Hope used two methods," she said. "She showed us the thoughtless words of Mr. Sanders and how that makes Paul feel," she said. "Also, Hope shows us Paul acting (5) ______________________________ toward Mr. Sanders."

Hannah's example followed Hope's.

The Setting and Situation: The Throne Room of the palace where peasants are coming to present their requests to the queen.

The young man slowly approached the throne with his hat in his hand and his eyes downcast. He bowed to the queen and addressed her by saying, "Your royal highness, I beg to ask your attention to the matter of my petition to hunt in the royal forest."

"I know," said Luke. The young man is acting (6) ______________________________, and Hannah shows the young peasant's seriousness through his actions and words."

Luke volunteered to be next.

The Setting and Situation: Two students are in the hall after math class.

"I can't believe Mr. Sanders called Paul lazy in front of the entire class," said Mandy.

"Agree," said Lynn. "I wonder how long he can get away with treating kids so disrespectfully."

Hope knew immediately. "Luke continued with my example," she said, "and he used others talking about Mr. Sanders. Mandy and Lynn wondered if Mr. Sanders was acting (7) ____________________ and possibly might be reported to the principal."

Celeste offered to give her example next.

The Setting and Situation: Two boys are fighting in the hallway during class exchange.

"Boys," said Mr. Spencer as he pulled the two apart, "come into my classroom and let's talk about what's going on."

Luke offered his answer. "Celeste showed through Mr. Spencer's words and actions that he acts (8) ____________________," he explained.

John gave the last example.

The Setting & Situation: Art class and the teacher has just explained the assignment to paint an interpretation of urban life.

"My painting will be of abstract shapes and forms that represent city life, and I think I'll use black, white, and gray for nonliving objects and orange for living things," thought Aaron.

Emmalin answered. "John showed Aaron's thoughts and from his thoughts we can see that he (9) ____________________ thinks about his art assignment."

As class ended Mr. Riley complimented his class on the excellent work of using the methods of characterization as well as the vocabulary words.

direct characterization - telling ☹

indirect characterization - showing ☺

**D.** The underlined part in each sentence is a synonym, idiom, phrase, or definition for a list word. Unscramble the list word and write the word on the blank.

1. The politician <u>dishonestly</u> told the people that she would lower their taxes if she was elected, with no intention of doing that. ____________________ leycuhlaint

2. Gary <u>unobtrusively</u> stood up and left the auditorium when he felt sick. ____________________ oyuopsinslicncu

3. Mrs. Bradley <u>hesitantly</u> boarded the roller coaster at Sea World during a class trip. ____________________ tucyrlateln

4. A group of girls <u>offensively</u> talked and laughed loudly during the symphony performance. ____________________ nsoxiuoyblo

5. Mr. Clark <u>wisely</u> postponed the social studies test when he learned that his students had an English research paper due on the same day. ____________________ isuydijlcuo

6. The bride and groom <u>seriously</u> promised that they would love and respect each other. ____________________ mlynselo

7. Becky's little brother, Charlie, <u>insolently</u> replied, "I don't feel like it," when she asked him to put his toys away. ____________________ niyptemltiner

8. Emmalin glanced <u>curiously</u> at Celeste who had her head down on her desk and her eyes closed. ____________________ nytisieuvliqi

9. Mrs. Bradley's science students <u>innovatively</u> worked on their bridge designs using only toothpicks and glue. ____________________ oieyiuglsnn

**E.** Write the word, idiom, or phrase from the choice box that best defines each list word.

- disrespectfully
- surly
- dignified
- wisely
- curiously
- immorally
- unpleasantly
- unnoticeably
- hesitantly
- creatively

1. reluctantly ______________________________

2. ingeniously ______________________________

3. impertinently ______________________________

4. solemnly ______________________________

5. inconspicuously ______________________________

6. obnoxiously ______________________________

7. inquisitively ______________________________

8. judiciously ______________________________

9. unethically ______________________________

**F.** Complete each sentence to show that you understand the meaning of the underlined word.

1. John inconspicuously entered the gym by ______________________________________________

   ______________________________________________.

2. "Your art assignment is to surprise me with an original sketch," said Ms. Steinman and ingeniously, Max drew ______________________________________________

   ______________________________________________.

3. While in the checkout line at the grocery store, the little boy impertinently

   ______________________________________________

   ______________________________________________.

4. When Milly asked her mother for permission to drive to Florida with her friends for Spring Break, her mom judiciously explained that ______________________________________________

   ______________________________________________.

5. When talking to Casey's parents during a conference, Mr. Zhang said, "He acted unethically by ______________________________________________

   ______________________________________________."

6. Solemnly the group of students ______________________________________________

   ______________________________________________.

7. Rachel reluctantly agreed to ______________________________________________

   ______________________________________________.

8. Mrs. Denby, the music teacher, asked Gary to apologize to Hope after he obnoxiously

   ______________________________________________

   ______________________________________________.

9. Inquisitively, Suzanne went to the library to ______________________________________________

   ______________________________________________.

# Vocabulary List 3
## Volatile Verbs

| Word<br>[pronunciation]<br>**other word form**<br> | Definition<br>• sample sentence<br> |
|---|---|
| **acknowledge**<br>[ak NOL ij]<br>**acknowledgement** (n) | [1]to admit the existence or truth of [2]to show appreciation for<br>• [1]Meteorologists acknowledged the danger of mud slides after the heavy rain.<br>• [2]Dylan sent a text message to his aunt acknowledging the birthday gift she sent. |
| **accost**<br>[uh KOST] | to approach and address someone in a bold or aggressive way<br>• Rachel's mother was accosted in the parking lot by a man demanding money. |
| **compensate**<br>[KOM puhn sayt]<br>**compensation** (n) | [1]to pay for work done, for something lost or damaged, or for some inconvenience [2]to adjust or make up for<br>• [1]Michael's father compensated the technologist who repaired his computer.<br>• [2]"Franny's bubbly personality compensates for her occasional brattiness," admitted Mandy about her little sister. |
| **decimate**<br>[DES uh meyt]<br>**decimation** (n) | to reduce drastically, especially in number<br>• The population of black rhinoceros in Africa has been nearly decimated because of hunting. |
| **defer**<br>[dih FUR] | to put off or to delay<br>• Casey's parents decided to defer their plans to move until the current school year ended. |
| **justify**<br>[JUHS tuh fahy]<br>**justification** (n) | to show to be just or right<br>• "Nothing justifies cheating on a test," admonished Mrs. Cole. |
| **litigate**<br>[LIHT ih geyt]<br>**litigation** (n) | using the judicial process to decide and settle something<br>• The Supreme Court is the highest U.S. federal court where important cases are litigated. |
| **malign**<br>[muh LIYN] | to speak about or criticize in a harmful way<br>• The food critic maligned the reputation of the new restaurant by saying the food was inedible and the service was inferior. |
| **obfuscate**<br>[ob fuhs keyt]<br>**obfuscation** (n) | to make obscure or unclear<br>• Old English was the earliest recorded English language from circa 1150 A.D. and is obfuscated by ancient spelling. |

**A.** Write the best list word that the synonyms, idioms, or phrases define to complete each sentence.

| | | | |
|---|---|---|---|
| compensate | accosted | justified | malign |
| acknowledged | decimated | litigate | obfuscating |
| confer | defer | compensated | acknowledged |

1. Historians ____________________ the Roman emperor Nero for disregarding the welfare of his people, executing anyone he didn't trust, and plotting to kill his own mother.

   slandered vilified cast aspersions on denigrated

2. Each morning Casey tried to ____________________ getting up by pushing the snooze button on his alarm clock.

   postpone suspend table put off

3. As Hillary's mom tried to enter the grocery store, she was ____________________ by angry picketers carrying signs demanding fair wages.

   confronted waylaid detained bothered

4. People finally ____________________ that the world was round after Ferdinand Magellan and his Spanish fleet made the first circumnavigation of Earth in 1519.

   accepted recognized allowed conceded

5. Max was ____________________ for the overtime hours he worked at the fast-food restaurant.

   recompensed reimbursed remunerated paid

6. Dylan ____________________ coming late for class by telling Mrs. Bradley that he neglected to adjust his alarm clock for daylight savings time.

   explained defended accounted for vindicated

7. The Deepwater Horizon oil spill in the Gulf of Mexico in 2010 ____________________ many species of marine wildlife.

   wiped out annihilated exterminated obliterated

8. A person on trial can avoid perjury charges for ____________________ the truth by pleading the Fifth Amendment, which protects a witness from giving testimony that might lead to self-incrimination.

   baffling befuddling obscuring perplexing

9. An increase in precipitation is needed to ______________________ for the increased dryness because of global warming.

make amends atone make reparation

10. When lawyers ______________________, they usually focus on a certain type of law such as criminal law or tax law.

prosecute press charges file suit contest

11. At a school assembly, Principal Zhang ______________________ the work that Mrs. Bradley's science class did creating posters encouraging recycling.

expressed gratitude thanked gave credit praised

**B.** Write the best word from the choice box to complete each sentence.

| litigation | malign | acknowledgement | obfuscation |
|---|---|---|---|
| accosted | fabricate | decimation | defer |
| compensation | justification | | |

1. The US Gulf Coast was left in ______________________________ after being struck by Hurricane Katrina in 2005.

2. Emmalin's ______________________________ that she was the one responsible for forgetting to lock the front door resulted in a reminder about home safety concerns.

3. As ______________________________ for his nearsightedness, Christopher wore special prescription glasses.

4. "You may not like someone, but it's not an excuse to ______________________________ him or her to others," warned Principal Zhang.

5. " ______________________________ of the main issues occurs when irrelevant arguments are added to persuasive essays," reminded Ms. Paterson.

6. Following the minor car collision, the two parties involved decided to settle the matter between them rather than resort to ______________________________.

7. Bernie's ______________________________ for playing video games was that he had just spent eight hours working on his research paper.

8. While biking on the trail, Dylan was ______________________________ by two boys who assaulted him and stole his bike.

9. When Mr. Stewart announced that he would ______________________________ the literature test until after Winter Break, everyone cheered.

## C. Story Challenge

Write the best word from the choice box to fill each blank in the story.

| | | | |
|---|---|---|---|
| acknowledged | obliterate | defer | justify |
| decimated | litigating | compensated | compensate |
| malign | acknowledged | accosted | obfuscate |

### To Make a Long Story Short

"It's raining cats and dogs," complained Julia as she entered Ms. Paterson's class. "I got drenched just running from the car to the school door." The others (1) ______________________________ her complaint, muttering about the third rainy day in a row.

"If you happened to hear Julia when she came into the room, you know the focus of today's lesson," said Ms. Paterson after all the kids were seated. "She used an idiom and we'll be discussing idioms today. I'll begin by telling you the origin of Julia's idiom," she continued. "Once, long ago, houses had thatched roofs with thick straw piled high and no wood underneath. Cats, dogs, mice, bugs, and other small animals lived in the straw on the roof, because it was the only place of warmth. With rain, the straw became slippery and sometimes the animals would slip and fall off the roof."

"So, it really would rain cats and dogs," confirmed Dylan.

Ms. Paterson continued, "The word idiom comes from the Greek 'idios,' which means personal. Idioms are personal words and phrases that are used by a particular group of people. Someone from Pennsylvania might use an idiom that possibly wouldn't be recognized by a California native. Or we may see an idiom in a Shakespearean play that we don't understand in the 21st century. Idioms can often (2) ____________________ word meanings for those trying to learn a different language. Nearly every country and historical age has its own idioms."

"Someone (3) ______________________________ me on my way to the auditorium for the dress rehearsal of *Our Town*, and said to break a leg. I know that idiom is a wish for good luck or to do well in a play, but I don't know the origin," said Tim.

"I know that one," said Ms. Paterson. "In medieval times some people believed in sprites—spirits or ghosts that were believed to enjoy causing trouble. So, the thought was that if a sprite heard you ask for something—it would try to make the opposite happen," explained Ms. Paterson.

"I get it," said Bernie. "Sort of like reverse Middle Ages psychology. So, break a leg means be careful so you don't break your leg."

"The other day," said Cindy, "even with asthma, I was able to (4) ________________ joining the tennis team when the doctor said he could give me a clean bill of health after my physical exam. Is 'clean bill of health' an idiom?" asked Cindy.

"Long ago," explained Ms. Paterson, "the hold of a ship sailing from a port would be (5) ____________________________ if the ship didn't have an official document declaring that there was no epidemic or infection present on the ship. This document was called a Bill of Health."

"I have an example of an idiom that my dad always uses, but I don't know the origin," said Suzanne. "He says, 'Don't count your chickens before they're hatched.' He means that you should (6) ____________________________ your excitement about something until it actually happens," explained Suzanne.

"That idiom dates all the way back to Aesop in ancient Greece. *The Milkmaid and the Pail*, is a fable about a young girl carrying a pail of milk on her head and dreaming about what she would do with the milk—first making cream and butter to sell, and then with the profits, buying eggs and then the eggs would hatch into chickens, and then the chickens would lay eggs, etc. As you may guess, the milkmaid accidentally trips and all of her milk spills," Ms. Paterson concluded.

"On a TV courtroom drama, the defendant promised to change his behavior, and the judge who was (7) ____________________________ the case, said that actions speak louder than words," said Christopher. Where did that idiom originate?"

"We can go back to the Bible for the origin of that idiom," said Ms. Paterson. "In the New Testament John said '…let us not love with word or tongue, but in deed and truth.'"

"Yesterday, I asked Kara if she needed some help finishing her science research paper, and she (8) ____________________________ my offer to help by thanking me and then answered, 'I have so much else to do, that I'll cross that bridge when I come to it,'" said Piper.

Ms. Paterson also knew the origin of that idiom. "In the 1800s, crossing bridges was risky business. The traveler on foot or horseback could not rely on the condition of the bridge or even if the bridge still remained, until he or she arrived at the bridge," Ms. Paterson explained.

"I heard a girl (9) ____________________________ the dress that another girl wore to the dance, and the girl said she planned to give the girl who insulted her dress, a taste of her own medicine," said Julia. "I think that's an idiom."

"Yes," affirmed Ms. Paterson. I'm not sure of the origin of that idiom, but it would be interesting to find out.

Casey had his hand up. "When I accidentally dropped Aiden's cell phone that I borrowed and the case shattered, Aiden said, 'Dude, my phone cost an arm and a leg. I hope you're planning to (10) ______________________________ me.' I'm pretty sure Aiden was using an idiom."

"Yes, indeed," laughed Ms. Paterson. "Did you get another phone for Aiden?"

"No, but I (11) ______________________________ him by giving him the new iPad that I got for my birthday, which was more expensive than a new cell phone," said Casey.

"Be on the alert when you hear an idiom and if it arouses your curiosity, take some time and find out the origin of the word or phrase," suggested Ms. Paterson. As class ended, Ms. Paterson said, "You don't have to burn the midnight oil, but remember you do have a vocabulary quiz tomorrow."

More Interesting Idioms

- a penny for your thoughts
- barking up the wrong tree
- can't judge a book by its cover
- beat around the bush
- best thing since sliced bread

 

**D.** The underlined part in each sentence is a synonym, idiom, phrase, or definition for a list word. Unscramble the list word and write the word on the blank.

1. When Dylan and Danny accidentally broke their neighbor's garage window while playing baseball, they <u>made reparation</u> by paying to have the window replaced. ______________ nemactsdope

2. Mrs. Berkabile, the school librarian, <u>thanked</u> the students who gave her birthday cards on her special day. ______________ dklgdaneweco

3. Everyone breathed a sigh of relief when Mrs. Bradley <u>postponed</u> the due date for science projects until after Spring Break. ______________ efdredre

4. An attorney representing the school appeared in court to <u>press charges</u> against the perpetrator who had stolen computers from the library. ______________ aiteltig

5. "The thesis of your essay is <u>obscured</u> by irrelevant examples to support your main point," criticized Ms. Paterson when she conferenced with Ned about his writing. ______________ sefutabdoc

6. Casey finally <u>admitted</u> that Bella was exceptional in basketball when she made 13 out of 15 free-throw shots in gym class. ______________ endalceogkdw

7. With the money that Mr. Sherman <u>remunerated</u> Harvey for cutting his lawn during the summer, Harvey purchased a new iPhone. ______________ peomcnsedta

8. The structures in the small Kansas town in the path of the tornado were <u>annihilated</u>, but fortunately all of the people escaped harm by using underground shelters. ______________ ecidtemda

9. In a debate, with good reasons, Christopher <u>defended</u> his position that the school should adopt a uniform dress code. ______________ tsfeidjiu

10. The politician lost votes because voters resented the fact that he tried to <u>vilify</u> his opponent's reputation by telling half truths about him. ______________ ganlmi

11. Ms. Palmer <u>confronted</u> Luke in the hallway and asked him if he had scribbled graffiti on his desk in her room. ______________ ecadotcs

**E.** Write the word, idiom, or phrase from the choice box that best defines each list word.

- slander
- vindicate
- make amends for
- galvanize
- postpone
- exterminate
- prosecute
- waylay
- obscure
- to admit existence of
- reimburse
- to thank
- to invent

1. acknowledge ______________________
2. decimate ______________________
3. defer ______________________
4. malign ______________________
5. acknowledge ______________________
6. litigate ______________________
7. compensate ______________________
8. justify ______________________
9. accost ______________________
10. compensate ______________________
11. obfuscate ______________________

**F.** Complete each sentence to show that you understand the meaning of the underlined word.

1. On Father's Day, Brendan acknowledged his father by ______________________________
______________________________________________________________.

2. To malign someone's good name is morally wrong because ______________________________
______________________________________________________________.

3. Mrs. Paterson's comments were obfuscated by ______________________________
______________________________________________________________.

4. A man accosted Aiden in the school parking lot and asked him ______________________________
______________________________________________________________.

5. Michael explained to his physics teacher that his late assignment was justified because
______________________________________________________________.

6. The Mock Trial Club attended an actual trial where a case involving ____________________
______________________________________________ was being litigated.

7. Justin was forced to acknowledge that Max was the more talented chess player when
______________________________________________________________.

8. To compensate Suzanne for the book she had borrowed and lost, Mandy ________________
______________________________________________________________.

9. The tsunami decimated ______________________________________________
______________________________________________________________.

10. When it began to rain, the ______________________________________________
was deferred until ______________________________________________.

11. To compensate for the loss of sight, blind people sometimes ______________________________
______________________________________________________________.

# Vocabulary List 4
## Audacious Adjectives

| **Word**<br>[pronunciation]<br>**other word form** | **Definition**<br>• sample sentence |
|---|---|
|  |  |
| **copious**<br>[KOH pee uhs] | abundant in supply or quantity<br>• Hannah took copious notes during Mrs. Bradley's lecture about cell structure. |
| **culinary**<br>[KUHL uh ner ee] | related to the kitchen or cooking<br>• Dylan's older brother Danny, who wished to become a chef, planned to attend the Culinary Institute of America in New York, NY. |
| **ebullient**<br>[ih BUHL yunt]<br>**ebullience** (n) | overflowing with cheerfulness, enthusiasm, or excitement<br>• Ms. Palmer was a consistently ebullient teacher. |
| **frugal**<br>[FROO guhl]<br>**frugality** (n) | showing economy in the use of money and/or resources<br>• Max was frugal and saved most of his money for a down payment on a car. |
| **grandiose**<br>[GRAN dee ohs]<br>**grandiosity** (n) | excessively grand or ambitious<br>• The architect's grandiose plans did not consider budget constraints. |
| **heterogeneous**<br>[het er uh JEE nee uhs] | consists of diverse or incongruous elements<br>• The neighborhood was a mix of heterogeneous ethnic groups. |
| **homogeneous**<br>[hoh muh JEE nee uhs] | of the same kind or nature<br>• The audience at the opera was a homogeneous grouping of Verdi fans. |
| **immutable**<br>[ih MYOO tuh buhl]<br>**immutability** (n) | unchanging over time or unable to be changed<br>• The laws of physics are thought to be immutable. |
| **obsequious**<br>[uhb SEE kwee uhs] | too eager to please someone, often in an insincere way<br>• The waiter's obsequious behavior was annoying. |

**A.** Write the best list word that the synonyms, idioms, or phrases define to complete each sentence.

| | | | |
|---|---|---|---|
| copious | grandiose | homogeneous | obsequious |
| ebullient | culinary | immutable | mawkish |
| frugal | heterogeneous | | |

1. A/An ______________________________ group of presidential advisors would not be healthy; the commander-in-chief needs diverse points of view.

   alike equal comparable uniform

2. "You owe me another penny," said the ____________________________ Suzanne when Julia paid her back for the lunch money she had borrowed.

   parsimonious miserly stingy penurious

3. "Your wish is my command," declared the king's ____________________________ attendant as he bowed deeply.

   brown-nosing deferential groveling ingratiating

4. The new restaurant did not try to be ____________________________, but instead offered delicious food in a simple, minimalist setting.

   pretentious showy bombastic ostentatious

5. The laws of physics, such as the speed of light, are ______________________________.

   enduring perpetual permanent inflexible

6. A/An ____________________________ group of dogs romped in the waves and chased balls, Frisbees, and each other at Dog Beach in Oceanside, California.

   assorted diversified disparate motley

7. Emmalin attracted a/an ______________________________ number of friends because of her friendly, jovial personality.

   ample bountiful plentiful profuse

8. Hannah's sister Lucy, a successful swimmer, was in a/an ____________________________ mood after she was offered a scholarship to attend Stanford University, one of the top 10 Division 1 schools for women's swimming.

   exuberant effervescent zestful vivacious

9. "My ____________________________ repertoire includes peanut butter and jelly sandwiches, and mac and cheese out of a box," joked Ned.

   edible savory palatable appetizing

 

**B.** Write the best word from the choice box to complete each sentence.

| | | | |
|---|---|---|---|
| frugality | nebulous | obsequious | grandiosity |
| copious | culinary | heterogeneous | ebullience |
| homogeneous | immutability | | |

1. Mandy's ___________________________ was the opposite of the humility of her best friend Kara.

2. Celeste's mother credited her expertise in cooking to the lessons she took at the Escoffier _______________________ School in Boulder, Colorado.

3. When Gary's father lost his job because of budget cuts, their family had to practice ___________________________ with money.

4. No matter what the circumstances, Emmalin's ___________________________ was apparent, as though she couldn't repress her exuberant spirit.

5. "'Will you walk into my parlor?' said the spider to the fly." The cunning spider tries to ensnare the naïve fly through the ___________________________ behavior of seduction and flattery in Mary Howitt's poem, "The Spider and the Fly".

6. Some educators believe that a/an __________________________ grouping of students is advisable for reasons such as giving opportunities for peer tutoring and improving student acceptance of differences.

7. Some scientists continually seek to discover _________________________ in the laws of nature while others challenge any assumptions.

8. Bella received a/an ____________________________ amount of flowers, balloons, and get-well wishes from her teachers and classmates when she was in the hospital for surgery.

9. In elementary school, teachers often use ______________________________ grouping, placing students in reading groups according to level and ability.

 

## C. Story Challenge

Write the best word from the choice box to fill each blank in the story.

| | | | |
|---|---|---|---|
| immutable | mawkish | homogeneous | ebullient |
| frugal | copious | grandiose | obsequious |
| heterogeneous | culinary | | |

## Playing With Puns

Milly entered her classroom in a/an (1)____________________________ mood because she was excited about sharing the information she discovered about the idiom, it cost an arm and a leg. Meanwhile, Caroline was teasing Michael who had asked to borrow some paper and a pencil. "Surely, you have supplies today," she laughed. "You borrowed paper and a pencil from Elsie yesterday."

"First of all, my name isn't Shirley," Michael joked. "And furthermore, I'm only asking you because you are so beautiful and generous, and incidentally your hair looks so shiny today."

"Your (2)______________________________ words are not helping your cause, Michael," chided Caroline.

"Class, enough bantering," reminded Ms. Paterson. "I have a/an (3)___________________________ amount of material I want to cover today, but first I want Milly to tell us the origin of the idiom, it cost an arm and a leg."

"This is so interesting," said Milly. "One theory is that long ago the least expensive, or the most (4)__________________________ choice of a portrait that a client could order to be painted was a head and shoulders portrait. The next highest priced portrait was one that included arms, and the very highest priced portrait— the most (5)_____________________________ option, was a 'legs and all' portrait. Thus the idiom—it cost an arm and a leg."

"Milly, I'm thrilled that you did extra research about idioms. And, Michael, did you realize you were using a pun in your conversation with Caroline about borrowing some supplies?"

"I was? What's a pun?" asked Michael.

"A pun is a play on words in which a humorous effect is produced by using a word that suggests two or more meanings. So, when Caroline, said, 'Surely, you have supplies today,' and Michael, when you replied that my name isn't Shirley, you were using a pun," explained Ms. Paterson.

"Puns are used in everyday life, often accidentally, but sometimes to make a joke or to try to be witty. For example, a/an (6)____________________________ pun might be the following," and Ms. Paterson wrote the pun on the board, so the students could see the spelling. Take the dough…I don't knead it.

"Two words—dough and knead have double meanings," observed Matt.

"Shakespeare was a master craftsman of puns and often used them in his plays," added Ms. Paterson. "Often, he used puns to give comic relief to a tragedy. For example, in *Romeo and Juliet*, the character Mercutio frequently uses puns in his conversation; he even uses a pun as he is dying after he has been stabbed by Tybalt. 'Tomorrow, you shall find me a grave man,' are his dying words. His use of grave has two meanings—grave meaning serious or the place where a body is buried," explained Ms. Paterson.

"I have an example," said John. "First of all, the animals on the African savannah are a/an (7)____________________________ group—from the tiny meerkat to the huge elephant. So, imagine a lion greeting some other animals on the savannah. The lion says, 'Pleased to eat you,'" said John.

"I have one about animals also," said Mandy. "My example is about a/an (8)____________________________ grouping of fish. 'Why are fish so smart? Because they live in schools,'" offered Mandy.

"Good examples, John and Mandy. Brendan, you look eager to give an example."

"We learned in science class that the basic particles that make up atoms—protons, neutrons, and electrons—are (9)____________________________. A hydrogen atom is the simplest atom that contains a single positive-charged proton in the nucleus, orbited by a single negative-charged electron. So, my example has to do with hydrogen atoms. Two hydrogen atoms meet. One says, "I've lost my electron." The other says, "Are you sure?" The first replies, "Yes, I'm positive."

"Good work today, class," said Ms. Paterson as class ended, "and remember, Time flies like an arrow. Fruit flies like a banana."

**Culinary Puns**

- I relish the fact that you've mustard the strength to ketchup to me.
- What is a thesaurus' favorite dessert? Synonym buns

**D.** The underlined part in each sentence is a synonym, idiom, phrase, or definition for a list word. Unscramble the list word and write the word on the blank.

1. "My dad is <u>parsimonious</u>," complained Dylan. "My allowance is $10 a week, and most of my friends get $20 weekly." ________________ glafur

2. The interests of Cindy's friends are <u>alike</u>; they all like science and math and avidly read dystopian fiction. ________________ esoemognhuo

3. Hannah is <u>deferential</u> to her older sister Lucy and does all she can to impress Lucy and make her proud. ________________ qisoseuobu

4. "Aiden should show a little humility instead of being so <u>ostentatious</u> and bragging about how smart he is," advised Caroline. ________________ sdrigenoa

5. Emmalin, in her usual <u>vivacious</u> way, warmly greeted her teammates with high-fives as they gathered in the gym to play volleyball. ________________ lnbiuetel

6. Mrs. Berkabile has a <u>plentiful</u> collection of contemporary young adult fiction in the library. ________________ ospucio

7. Principal Zhang invited a <u>diversified</u> group of students from all classes and all interests to discuss ways to boost school spirit. ________________ soeheugetnero

8. Dylan's brother Danny, who loved to cook, created <u>palatable</u> delights for family dinners such as chicken coq a vin. ________________ luynrcia

9. Principal Zhang emphasized that treating all others with respect is a/an <u>permanent</u> part of the school policy. ________________ temluimba

**E.** Write the word, idiom, or phrase from the choice box that best defines each list word.

- stingy
- equal
- unsettling
- bombastic
- savory
- disparate
- plentiful
- fawning
- effervescent
- perpetual

1. heterogeneous ______________________________

2. grandiose ______________________________

3. obsequious ______________________________

4. culinary ______________________________

5. homogeneous ______________________________

6. ebullient ______________________________

7. immutable ______________________________

8. frugal ______________________________

9. copious ______________________________

**F.** Complete each sentence to show that you understand the meaning of the underlined word.

1. Many elementary schools choose to use <u>heterogeneous</u> groupings of students in classes because ______________________________________________.

2. The audience at the symphony was a <u>homogeneous</u> grouping of ____________________ ____________________________________________________________.

3. We could tell she had a <u>grandiose</u> sense of self-importance by ______________________ ____________________________________________________________.

4. To convince her mother to let her go to the party with her friends, Hope resorted to <u>obsequious</u> behavior by ____________________________________________________ ____________________________________________________________.

5. One skill Chris learned in the <u>culinary</u> class that he took during the summer was ____________________________________________________________.

6. John took <u>copious</u> notes in history class about ___________________________________ ____________________________________________________________.

7. Bella said an <u>immutable</u> rule in her family is _____________________________________ ____________________________________________________________.

8. At her party, the <u>ebullient</u> birthday girl, Hillary, greeted her guests by _________________ ____________________________________________________________.

9. Because he had been <u>frugal</u> with money he earned and received as gift, Dylan __________ ____________________________________________________________.

# Review: Lists 1-4

**A.** Use the clues to complete the crossword puzzle with vocabulary words, synonyms, or information from the activities.

**Across**

1. Show appreciation
4. An effervescent person would be ________
5. Career of a culinary expert
8. All the same
10. Slander
11. Abundant
12. Frugal

**Down**

1. Approach in a bold way
2. Cheerful
3. Diverse
6. Equal to
7. Unchangeable

**B.** Circle the answer which best completes the sentence.

1. The teacher **judiciously**
   a. ate three doughnuts.
   b. settled the dispute.
   c. passed out the tests.

2. The **frugal** man
   a. refused to spend money on trivial items.
   b. reconciled with his girlfriend.
   c. dropped his cell phone.

3. He **reluctantly**
   a. approached the snarling dog.
   b. ate the cake and ice cream.
   c. accepted the cash prize.

4. **Impertinently**, the girl
   a. wrote a thank-you note to her aunt.
   b. talked loudly during the symphony.
   c. worked on her science project.

5. An **obsequious** person would
   a. grovel.
   b. sing a song.
   c. order French fries.

6. Her ski vacation plans were **decimated** when
   a. she ordered food for the party.
   b. she received an A+ on her essay.
   c. she fell and broke her leg.

7. A **grandiose** person might
   a. get a prescription filled.
   b. have a picnic in the park.
   c. brag about a victory.

8. **Solemnly**, he
   a. blew up the balloons.
   b. approached the witness stand.
   c. danced the jitterbug.

9. **Obnoxiously**, he
   a. quietly took his seat.
   b. had a Caesar salad for lunch.
   c. talked with his mouth full.

10. A quality of a **perspicacious** person is
    a. understanding.
    b. shallowness.
    c. musical talent.

11. The best place to **litigate** is
    a. during a hockey game.
    b. in a courtroom.
    c. in your dreams.

12. He was **compensated** for
    a. getting a failing grade on a test.
    b. weeding the garden.
    c. forgetting his book.

**C.** From the list of fictional book titles, write the best word that might be used in each book.

| | | | |
|---|---|---|---|
| unethically | truculent | obfuscate | spurious |
| banal | mawkish | justify | inconspicuously |
| acknowledge | ingeniously | surreptitious | inquisitively |
| visceral | | | |

1. ______________________ *Movies and Songs to Make you Shed Tears*

2. ______________________ *Curiosity About the World Around Us*

3. ______________________ *Wall Street Corruption*

4. ______________________ *Thinking Creatively*

5. ______________________ *Controlling Anger and Rage*

6. ______________________ *How Not to Make a Fool of Yourself*

7. ______________________ *Can You Trust Your Intuition?*

8. ______________________ *Why the Constitution Should Be Changed*

9. ______________________ *Peace Obscured by Factions Vying for Power in the Middle East*

10. ______________________ *False Claims by the Defendant Lead to Conviction*

11. ______________________ *When Scientists Admitted the World Was Round*

12. ______________________ *Clandestine Operations of the CIA*

# Vocabulary List 5
## Academic Adjectives

| **Word**<br>[pronunciation]<br>**other word form**<br> | **Definition**<br>• sample sentence<br> |
|---|---|
| **autodidactic**<br>[aw toh diy DAK tik]<br>**autodidact** (n) | relating to or having the characteristics of a self-taught person<br>• The autodidactic learner has a vast collection of books in his study. |
| **banal**<br>[buh NAHL]<br>**banality** (n) | containing nothing new, original, or unusual<br>• A banal essay would not impress an English teacher. |
| **clandestine**<br>[klan DES tin] | characterized by or done with secrecy or concealment<br>• CIA operatives had a clandestine meeting in Berlin. |
| **disconcerting**<br>[dis kuhn SUR ting] | a feeling of worry, confusion, or surprise<br>• Supposedly, Santa Ana winds can cause a disconcerting feeling. |
| **egalitarian**<br>[ih gal ih TAIR ee uhn]<br>**egalitarianism** (n) | belief in the political, economic, and social equality of all people<br>• An egalitarian person would not be biased. |
| **infallible**<br>[in FAL uh buhl]<br>**infallibility** (n) | perfect, trustworthy, or flawless<br>• Science is not infallible and theories change with new discoveries. |
| **nebulous**<br>[NEB yuh luhs] | hazy, cloudy, fuzzy<br>• Nebulous writing lacks clarity. |
| **peripatetic**<br>[per uh puh TET ik] | traveling frequently from place to place<br>• The life of a salesperson can be peripatetic. |
| **stoic**<br>[STOH ik]<br>**stoicism** (n) | someone who accepts things without emotion or complaint<br>• She remained stoic throughout her chemotherapy treatments. |

**A.** Decide if the underlined words are used correctly in the sentences below. Write Correct or Incorrect on the blank.

1. ______________________________ His banal essay was creative and interesting.

2. ______________________________ She was infallible and frequently made mistakes in her writing.

3. ______________________________ The stoic prisoner withstood threats and frequent beatings without confessing to crimes he did not commit.

4. ______________________________ Her directions were so nebulous that we got lost and arrived at the movie theater an hour late.

5. ______________________________ As an autodidactic learner, he took classes in Analytical Geometry, French, Literature, and Western Philosophy.

6. ______________________________ Mom had disconcerting feelings about driving to the airport in a big snowstorm.

7. ______________________________ Even though Aiden tried to be clandestine, his father found out he was going to his friend's house instead of to the library to study.

8. ______________________________ His egalitarian beliefs included the idea that men were more qualified than women to work in the business world.

9. ______________________________ The peripatetic elderly gentleman rarely left his little apartment.

**B.** Write the best word from the choice box to complete each sentence.

| | | | |
|---|---|---|---|
| autodidact | peripatetic | disconcerting | infallibility |
| nebulous | stoicism | clandestine | egalitarianism |
| immutable | banality | | |

1. Aiden's family found the information that bears roam freely in the area where they planned to camp very ______________________________.

2. Mr. Clark explained that in the mid 1800s, Susan B. Anthony campaigned for ______________________________—the right of men and women to study, live, and work as equals.

3. Because his answers to his opponent's questions in the cross-examination were ______________________________, Ms. Palmer criticized Brian's debate performance.

4. Mrs. Berkabile, the middle-school librarian, boasted that Ray Bradbury, the famous author of fantasy, horror, science fiction, and mystery novels was a/an ______________________________ who credited libraries for his learning. He once said, "When I graduated from high school, it was during the Depression and we had no money for college, so I went to the library for three days a week for ten years."

5. Mr. Stewart suggested that perfectionists should read The Shel Silverstein poem, "Almost Perfect" about the dangers of thinking that ______________________________ is a human quality.

6. In his book report about Robert Louis Stevenson's classic novel *The Strange Case of Dr. Jekyll and Mr. Hyde*, Brendan explained that the respected Doctor Jekyll, in a/an ______________________________ way, is transformed into the violent and cruel Mr. Hyde.

7. Dylan's older brother Danny hoped to find a job as a pharmacist so he could settle down in one place, rather than work as a/an ____________________________ salesman for a drug company.

8. Mr. Clark said that the ancient Greeks believed that a person with ____________________________ was one who exercised self-control and courage, and did not allow emotions such as anger or jealousy to cloud judgment.

9. As a candidate for student government president, Gary did not address the real issues about which the students were concerned, but instead resorted to __________________________, using the same old talking points about more free days and less homework.

## C. Story Challenge

Write the best word from the choice box to fill each blank in the story.

| | | | |
|---|---|---|---|
| autodidactic | egalitarian | stoic | disconcerting |
| infallible | clandestine | peripatetic | nebulous |
| banal | heterogeneous | | |

## Vocabulary in Action

Mr. Stewart had nine new vocabulary words listed on the board. He gave his students thirty minutes to choose one of the words, connect the word to something personal, and then to write about it. Mr. Stewart provided an example.

"I recall about two years ago," he began, "it was July, and I was arriving home from a two-week vacation in Bermuda. As I opened my front door, I noticed the lights on. I had a very (1)______________________________ feeling because I knew I had checked and rechecked the lights before leaving the house. As I walked further into the house, it was obvious that an intruder had been there. The contents of a bookcase were dumped on the floor, and drawers were hanging open."

"Then I would continue my writing by telling what happened next," he explained.

"No fair," Mr. Stewart," complained the class. "You can't be so (2)______________________________ about the details. We want to hear the rest of the story."

Mr. Stewart promised he would finish the story later and the class began to write. Twenty minutes later Mr. Stewart asked for volunteers to discuss what they had written. Hope said that she wrote about her difficulty with writing and how often her writing seems (3)______________________________, instead of being interesting. She continued by saying she admired the composition skills of Milly and Aiden, both of whom had displayed a definite writing talent.

Aiden was not (4)______________________________ about how he enjoyed writing. He openly shared his poetry, memoirs, stories, and plays with his classmates. "How did you learn to be such a good writer?" Hope asked him.

"I am somewhat of a/an (5)______________________________ learner when it comes to writing," explained Aiden. "I never took a special writing class," he said. "I just practice by journaling every day and also, I'm an avid reader—of both poetry and prose. By reading works of other authors and poets, I learn many techniques of writing. "But Hope," he encouraged, "I wish I had your talent for math. Writing just happens to be one of my strengths and math is one of yours."

Next, Caroline shared her writing about her dream to someday be a/an (6)______________________________ traveler, backpacking all over the world. "I hope someday to see places like Timbuktu, Kenya, Iceland, and Japan—places I've enjoyed reading about," she wrote.

Dylan wrote about someone he considered a hero. "Senator John McCain," he read, "was taken prisoner during the war in Vietnam, and was (7)__________________________ as he endured pain and suffering for five years as a POW."

"I also wrote about someone I believe is a hero," said Mandy. "I learned about Elizabeth Cady Stanton in social studies class and how she believed in and fought for (8)______________________________ rights for all people."

"I wrote more of an opinion piece," explained Christopher. "I wrote about how most people try to be the best they can, but how mistakes are a part of life and part of the human learning experience. Therefore, I wrote about the impossibility of being totally (9)______________________________."

Everyone had the opportunity to share his or her writing, and the class ended with a promise from Mr. Stewart to later continue the story about when his home was burglarized.

Famous Autodidacts

- Alexander Graham Bell – American inventor
- Thomas Alva Edison – American inventor
- Andrew Carnegie – wealthy American industrialist
- Arthur C. Clarke – science fiction writer
- Charles Dickens – great English novelist

**D.** The underlined part in each sentence is a synonym, idiom, phrase, or definition for a list word. Unscramble the list word and write the word on the blank.

1. America was founded on equality principles and the Constitution confirms that belief. ____________ inaliegrata

2. According to a legend, Johnny Appleseed (John Chapman) was a/an wandering American pioneer who spread apple seeds wherever he went. ____________ acitpeirpte

3. Emmalin, Becky, and Julia had a/an secret meeting to plan Hope's surprise birthday party. ____________ edecntiasln

4. "It is normal to have unsettling feelings before you have to give a speech," reminded Ms. Palmer. ____________ iecntdsginorc

5. After Celeste proofread her essay three times, she turned in what she hoped was a/an perfect paper. ____________ eiblflainl

6. Herman Melville, most famous for his novel, *Moby Dick*, was a self-taught learner who could not afford a college education, so therefore studied literature and philosophy on his own. ____________ tdicodacitua

7. Before they began writing personal narratives, Ms. Paterson reminded her students that stories with flat characters and a predictable ending were boring. ____________ nlaba

8. Mr. Clark taught his history class that the Spartans in ancient Greece were trained to be unemotional and uncomplaining. ____________ csito

9. Mr. Salter's math students were hazy about the date of the final test, so they asked him for clarification. ____________ obuslenu

**E.** Write the word, idiom, or phrase from the choice box that best defines each list word.

- commonplace
- obscure
- unemotional
- self-taught
- equitable
- flawless
- copious
- hush-hush
- disturbing
- frequent traveler

1. stoic ______________________________
2. clandestine ______________________________
3. peripatetic ______________________________
4. egalitarian ______________________________
5. nebulous ______________________________
6. disconcerting ______________________________
7. banal ______________________________
8. autodidactic ______________________________
9. infallible ______________________________

**F.** Complete each sentence to show that you understand the meaning of the underlined word.

1. Dylan, Aiden, and Tim planned a clandestine meeting to ______________________________

______________________________________________.

2. Ms. Paterson jotted the comment "banal" on Shane's essay and then explained her comment by saying ______________________________________________.

3. Becky considered herself an egalitarian person and wished for ______________________

______________________________________________.

4. As a peripatetic traveler, Ned's Aunt Brenda ______________________________

______________________________________________.

5. Milly had disconcerting feelings when______________________________

______________________________________________.

6. Everyone could tell Shane was a very stoic person when ______________________

______________________________________________.

7. "No one is infallible," said Christopher after he ______________________________

______________________________________________.

8. Max said he is an autodidactic art student and he learns by ______________________

______________________________________________.

9. Ms. Paterson instructed that one way in which nebulous writing could be improved is by

______________________________________________.

 

# Vocabulary List 6
## No-Nonsense Nouns

| **Word**<br>[pronunciation]<br>**other word form**<br> | **Definition**<br>• sample sentence<br> |
|---|---|
| **betrothal**<br>[bih TROH thul] | a formal agreement to marry<br>• Tim's older brother Owen had a party to announce his betrothal to his girlfriend Maureen. |
| **bravado**<br>[bruh VAH doh] | a show of boldness intended to impress or intimidate<br>• In a show of bravado, Luke volunteered to be the first to hold the boa constrictor. |
| **certitude**<br>[SUR ti tood] | absolute certainty or conviction that something is the case<br>• Hillary replied with certitude that her volleyball team would win their next game. |
| **conduit**<br>[KON doo it] | [1]a channel for protecting electric wires or for conveying water or other fluid [2]a means of transmitting or distributing<br>• [1]Conduit pipe for electric wires is made from both flexible and rigid materials.<br>• [2]The United States Postal System is a conduit for mail. |
| **demagogue**<br>[DEM uh gog]<br>**demagoguery** (n) | a leader who uses popular prejudices, false claims, and promises to gain power<br>• The senator's opponent called him a raving demagogue. |
| **hiatus**<br>[hiy AT us] | a pause or gap in activity, sequence, or process<br>• The students enjoyed a week's hiatus from school at Christmas. |
| **ichthyology**<br>[ik thee OL uh gee] | the branch of zoology that studies fish<br>• According to ichthyologists, the world's largest fish is the whale shark. |
| **mandate**<br>[MAN deyt] | a command to act in a certain way or to do something that is given by an authority<br>• Congress gave the president a mandate to send more troops into the region. |
| **pandemic**<br>[pan DEM ik] | a disease that is prevalent throughout an entire country, continent, or the whole world<br>• The Black Death of the 14th century was a pandemic that killed almost one-fourth of Europe's population. |

**A.** Write the word that best fits with the context of the sentence.

| | | | |
|---|---|---|---|
| conduit | certitude | ichthyology | betrothal |
| pandemic | conduit | demagogue | hiatus |
| bravado | mandate | gastronomy | |

1. The defendant was absolutely positive that he heard a gunshot between 2 a.m. and 2:30 a.m. ______________________________

2. The young couple celebrated their engagement with a party for family and friends.

   ______________________________

3. Emperor Augustus of Rome promised the people free grain and free entertainment such as chariot races and gladiators. ______________________________

4. Disinfectant was used to clean the pipes when the water had a rust taste.

   ______________________________

5. The U.S. President has the authority to release prisoners.

   ______________________________

6. Ms. Paterson planned to visit her daughter in Tampa, Florida, during spring break.

   ______________________________

7. The little Chihuahua barked ferociously at the German shepherd.

   ______________________________

8. The daily White House press conference provides the press with information about the activities and agenda of the U.S. President. ______________________________

9. HIV/AIDS, which originated in the Congo, is still being battled throughout the world.

   ______________________________

10. Piper and her family visited the Birch Aquarium in LaJolla, California.

   ______________________________

**B.** Write the best word from the choice box to complete each sentence.

| | | | |
|---|---|---|---|
| conduit | peripatetic | hiatus | pandemic |
| bravado | mandate | ichthyology | demagoguery |
| conduits | certitude | betrothal | |

1. Polio was a crippling, infectious ______________________ in the early 1900s.

2. "Snorkeling in Norman Reef in the Great Barrier Reef off the coast of Australia is like a lesson in ______________________," raved Max.

3. When Hannah went to the animal shelter, she knew with ______________________ that the beagle puppy with the sad brown eyes was the dog she wanted.

4. A sensible diet, adequate rest, and daily exercise are ______________________ leading to good health.

5. The politician was accused of ______________________ because he made promises that were impossible to keep.

6. After digging in the yard, the plumbers discovered a crack in the ______________________ that carried water to the sprinkler system.

7. Dylan's older brother Danny took a year's ______________________ after college and backpacked through Europe.

8. Everyone was surprised when Mr. Greenberg, the tennis coach, and Ms. Cosgrove, the gym teacher, announced their ______________________.

9. *The Americans with Disabilities Act* of 1990 was a federal ______________________ outlawing discrimination of any kind against anyone with a disability.

10. In a show of ______________________ David challenged the giant Goliath.

## C. Story Challenge

Write the best word from the choice box to fill each blank in the story.

| | | | |
|---|---|---|---|
| mandate | obscurity | hiatus | conduit |
| certitude | ichthyology | pandemic | demagogue |
| conduit | bravado | betrothal | |

### Jamming With Jargon

Ms. Paterson overheard the conversation of Cindy and Christopher as they took their seats. "We played doubles on Saturday," Chris said. "Hillary and I met at the court at The Tennis Club, and we played two matches against Mike and Kara, which was an act of (1)__________________________ for both of us, because those two usually soundly defeat any opponents. Hillary has this fantasy of someday being a Grand Slam winner like Serena Williams. She's trying to improve her stance, backhand, and follow-through."

After everyone was seated, Ms. Paterson said, "doubles, court, match, Grand Slam, stance, backhand, and follow-through. Tennis jargon is what Chris was using when he was talking to Cindy. Can anyone define jargon?"

"I think jargon is the special vocabulary used for a sport, a hobby, a profession, or just about anything," said Gary.

"You're correct, Gary," affirmed Ms. Paterson. "Class, look at the week's vocabulary list on the board. Do you see any nouns that might have a special vocabulary?"

"(2)__________________________," said Rachel. "My sister, Sarah, is engaged and plans to get married next year, so her dinner conversation is filled with wedding jargon such as bridesmaid, vows, maid of honor, cummerbund, tuxedo, veil, boutonniere, ring, and reception."

"I have an example," offered Justin. "My uncle Sid is a plumber, so I hear him use plumbing jargon such as "A" valve, (3)__________________________, and bleed, which in the plumbing world means to drain a pipe of excess air."

"(4)__________________________ also has specialized vocabulary such as adipose, dorsal fins, ichthyoplankton—meaning fish eggs and larvae—and benthic that means bottom dwelling," explained Ms. Paterson.

"Immunization, AIDS, antibody, antigens vaccine, communicable—can anyone identify the area for which these words might be considered jargon?" Ms. Paterson asked.

(5)"__________________________," Heidi said.

Next, Luke, who usually didn't volunteer to answer, replied with (6)__________________________. "Bases loaded, bush league, choke-up, clutch-hitter, bunt, and clean-up-hitter are all examples of jargon baseball players might use," Luke confidently announced.

"Excellent, Luke," complimented Ms. Paterson. Just then the chimes sounded, indicating that announcements would begin. The PA system at Jefferson was a/an (7)______________________________ for transmitting information to all the students. The students listened, enjoying the brief (8)______________________________ from the lesson. Following announcements, two students who were competing against each other for student government president were introduced by Principal Zhang, and they stated their promises of what each would do if elected.

"Brent sounds like a (9)______________________________," muttered Hillary. "How can he promise a four-day school week with a no-homework policy on weekends?" she criticized. "That would never happen."

Emmalin agreed, "He could never get a (10)______________________________ from the administration or the PTA to do the things he promises to do."

Just as announcements ended, class ended. "We'll continue our discussion of jargon tomorrow," said Ms. Paterson

.

Literary Jargon

- plot
- protagonist
- point of view
- conflict
- antagonist
- mood
- theme
- denouement
- exposition

**D.** The underlined part in each sentence is a synonym, idiom, phrase, or definition for a list word. Unscramble the list word and write the word on the blank.

1. In a car, gas reaches the engine through channels called fuel lines. ______ nusctdoi
2. The rabble-rouser incited the crowd by negative provocative statements about the government. ______ gmuegdoae
3. Rachel supported her contentions in debate with certainty because of strong, valid proof. ______ idueterct
4. The pep assembly in the gym provided an intermission from the routine class schedule. ______ uitsha
5. Principal Zhang gave his approval for students to organize a biology club. ______ anmtaed
6. With boldness, John's two miniature French poodles, growled and barked at the stranger at the door. ______ vobdara
7. Smallpox, a dangerous disease that once killed millions of people, has been wiped out thanks to global immunization. ______ dpeamcni
8. While engaged in the study of fish, Heidi learned that fish are divided into three classes, and the class called the Chondrocytes includes sharks, stingrays, and skates. ______ liycghtoyho
9. A picture of the happy couple and an article in the local paper publicly announced the engagement of Rachel's older sister Sarah and her fiancée Jeff. ______ ohbteltra
10. In 1835, Samuel Morse successfully developed a transmission method to send signals by wire using an electromagnet which moved a marker to produce written codes on a strip of paper. ______ dciount

**E.** Write the word, idiom, or phrase from the choice box that best defines each list word.

- widespread disease
- inconspicuous
- certainty
- unethical leader
- marriage agreement
- study of fish
- boastfulness
- channel for fluid or wires
- pause in activity
- means of communication
- official approval

1. conduit ____________________
2. certitude ____________________
3. mandate ____________________
4. pandemic ____________________
5. demagogue ____________________
6. bravado ____________________
7. conduit ____________________
8. ichthyology ____________________
9. betrothal ____________________
10. hiatus ____________________

**F.** Complete each sentence to show that you understand the meaning of the underlined word.

1. Their betrothal was announced by ______________________________

______________________________.

2. One thing the zoologist learned in his study of ichthyology is that ______________________________

______________________________.

3. The preferred conduit that teenagers use to communicate with friends is ______________________________

______________________________.

4. Principal Zhang issued the following mandate: ______________________________

______________________________.

5. At camp, with a show of bravado, Shane volunteered to ______________________________

______________________________.

6. Elsie said, "One thing I can say with certitude is ______________________________

______________________________."

7. The builders of the new home installed conduits for ______________________________

______________________________.

8. He exhibited the qualities of a demagogue when he ______________________________

______________________________.

9. One step that could be taken to stop a pandemic would be ______________________________

______________________________.

10. During the hiatus at the concert we ______________________________

______________________________.

# Vocabulary List 7
## Adventurous Adjectives

| **Word**<br>[pronunciation]<br>**other word form** | **Definition**<br>• sample sentence |
|---|---|
|  |  |
| **decadent**<br>[DEK uh duhnt]<br>**decadence** (n) | excessively indulgent in pleasure or luxury<br>• Some historians believe the fall of the Roman Empire was due in part to the decadence of Roman emperors and aristocrats. |
| **facetious**<br>[fuh SEE shuhs] | remarks that are not meant to be taken seriously<br>• John was being facetious when he told Bella she needed an attitude change, but unfortunately she took him seriously. |
| **garrulous**<br>[GAR uh luhs] | excessively talkative in a rambling, roundabout manner<br>• Harvey was garrulous, while his twin Hope was much more reserved. |
| **languid**<br>[LANG gwid] | lacking energy or enthusiasm<br>• Ned felt languid after running five miles during track practice. |
| **lucid**<br>[LOO sid]<br>**lucidity** (n) | expressed clearly in order to be easily understood<br>• "In a debate," instructed Ms. Palmer, "your goal is to speak in a convincing, lucid way." |
| **maritime**<br>[MAR ih tahym] | having to do with the sea<br>• Brendan's parents visited the Chesapeake Bay Maritime Museum in St. Michaels, Maryland, when they were on vacation. |
| **obstinate**<br>[OB stuh nit]<br>**obstinance** (n) | firmly or stubbornly adhering to one's purpose<br>• Milly's parents were obstinate about not allowing her to stop taking piano lessons. |
| **radical**<br>[RAD ih kuhl] | much more extreme than the usual or traditional<br>• Opposition to the war in Vietnam was a radical idea in the U.S. in the1960s. |
| **slanderous**<br>[SLAN der uhs]<br>**slander** (n) | false statements that damage another's reputation<br>• Abraham Lincoln once said that truth is the best revenge against slanderous talk. |

**A.** Decide if the underlined words are used correctly in the sentences below. Write Correct or Incorrect on the blank.

1. ______________________________ Ann enjoyed studying <u>maritime</u> ecology such as that of the Kalahari and Atacama deserts.

2. ______________________________ Ms. Paterson suggested that Becky redo her <u>lucid</u> essay for clarity.

3. ______________________________ Principal Zhang complimented Dylan for his <u>slanderous</u> remarks.

4. ______________________________ "Give your mouth a rest, Casey," teased Emmalin. "You're too <u>garrulous</u> today."

5. ______________________________ The hermit lived simply, enjoying his <u>decadent</u> lifestyle.

6. ______________________________ Max could always be counted on to have a <u>radical</u>, unique approach to any art assignment.

7. ______________________________ Celeste felt so <u>languid</u> that she took a nap instead of practicing piano.

8. ______________________________ Principal Zhang had a <u>facetious</u> discussion with Luke about his recent mean-spirited behavior.

9. ______________________________ Bernie was very <u>obstinate</u> and refused to let Dylan borrow his iPad.

**B.** Write the best word from the choice box to complete each sentence.

| | | | |
|---|---|---|---|
| obstinance | radical | lucidity | languid |
| garrulous | bravado | decadence | facetious |
| slander | maritime | | |

1. To many colonists, breaking ties with England was a ___________________________ idea.

2. "Oh, I just love rainy days," Caroline complained in a ___________________________ way when she came into class, dripping wet.

3. In a display of sweet ___________________________, the wedding banquet was laden with sumptuous desserts such as a chocolate fountain and a raspberry torte.

4. The four-year old twins for whom Hope baby sat were usually well-behaved, but demonstrated ___________________________ when it was time to go to bed

5. "Everyone enjoys your ___________________________ personality Brendan," chided Mr. Stewart. "However, now is the time for silence and serious study."

6. The U.S. Coast Guard Academy educates leaders of a ___________________________ military force and is located in New London, Connecticut.

7. Bella was ___________________________ and weak when she had the flu and had no desire for any activity.

8. In Shakespeare's *Othello*, Iago is guilty of ___________________________ when he falsely suggests that Othello's wife Desdemona has been unfaithful.

9. After he was involved in an accident and had to provide the details to a policewoman, Ned's ___________________________ was very surprising.

### C. Story Challenge

Write the best word from the choice box to fill each blank in the story.

| | | | |
|---|---|---|---|
| slanderous | iconic | lucid | languid |
| decadent | maritime | facetious | obstinate |
| garrulous | radical | | |

## Jargon Moves Next Door

Mr. Riley overheard yesterday's discussion about jargon. "Today," he said when his class was seated, "we'll borrow the idea of jargon to write a poem." Harvey, who was (1)____________________________ as usual, had to be reminded to end his conversation with Aiden, so that Mr. Riley could begin class.

"Aiden's using Renaissance jargon to tell me about today's history test," joked Harvey. The class, and even Mr. Riley laughed at Harvey's (2)_________________ retort.

"Harvey, you have the imagination and talent for poetry. I have a feeling you will appreciate today's assignment."

"That's (3)_________________________," joked Harvey. "I'm supposed to be a tennis jock. What will happen if I get a reputation as a poet?" he asked.

"Certainly the idea is not as (4)________________________ as you might think," said Mr. Riley. "From what I've learned, men with a sensitive side who write poetry are very attractive to others. In fact, General George S. Patton, a famous American general of WWII, wrote poetry on love as well as recording daily happenings in his pocket notebook."

"Your assignment for next class will be to write a poem using jargon. I'll read an example written by a student from last year's class. I still remember this student coming to class with an unusual (5)_________________________ demeanor, instead of his customary pep and vigor. Later, reading the poem that he composed that day, I understood his mood."

**Chance of Precipitation**

What happened?
from a balmy climate
with Chinook winds
sunshine with Celsius
in the 80s
to a feeling of Arctic air
a definite cold front moving in
bringing wind chill and smog
cumulonimbus clouds overhead
a definite La Nina
threatening to destroy
our relationship
Can you explain the permafrost?
Was it always there
just below the surface?
an ominous, portentous sign
predicting a chance
of precipitation

"I like that poem," complimented Shane. "The poet is very (6)_______________________ in expressing an idea. The weather jargon is perfect to communicate the idea of trouble in a relationship."

"You've heard me say so many times that good poetry comes from true emotion and experiences, and this student's poem is a good example," reminded Mr. Riley. "A jargon poem is a good way to show how you feel. For example, if you feel (7)_______________________ and self-indulgent because of someone or something, you might use the jargon of luxury, with words such as extravagance, hedonism, frills, riches, opulence, high-living, mansion, palatial, private jet, Maserati, and diamonds. On the other hand, if you were feeling like you were always being told what to do or what to think and you felt like rebelling and being (8)_______________________, maybe you could borrow some feline jargon such as tabby, claws, kitten, or litter, since cats are notorious for their stubborn refusal to yield to human demands," explained Mr. Riley. "I'll end with a/an (9)_______________________ example," said Mr. Riley. "I'm a sailor, so I'll use sailing jargon to describe the vicissitudes of life. Julia, you are our resident logophile, so can you review the meaning of vicissitudes?"

"For sure," said Julia. "As a word lover, I can tell you the word means the normal ups and downs of life."

Mr. Riley read his poem titled "Summer Squall."

A summer squall throws life out of whack
It blows in the form of a disappointment or a failure
Time to adjust the sails
Change the headsail if necessary
Keep on an even keel and do what is needed
to ride out the storm safely
The wind abates
The squall passes
Raise the sails, consider hoisting the spinnaker
Sail on
Knowing that sudden squalls
are a part of life

"Try a jargon poem and bring your efforts to our next class," said Mr. Riley, as class ended for the day.

Classic Maritime Novels

- *Moby Dick* by Herman Melville
- *20,000 Leagues Under the Sea* by Jules Verne
- *The Old Man and the Sea* by Ernest Hemingway
- *Two Years Before the Mast* by Richard Dana
- *The Captain Horatio Hornblower* Series by C.S. Forester

**D.** The underlined part in each sentence is a synonym, idiom, phrase, or definition for a list word. Unscramble the list word and write the word on the blank.

1. At lunch, when Caroline passed out the delicious chocolate-chip cookies she baked to celebrate Ann's birthday, Justin replied in a <u>flippant</u> way, "I hate these cookies, so I'll take two, just so you can get rid of them." ____________ stofaicue

2. Many people in foreign nations, who only know America from movies and television, believe the people are all <u>indulgent</u>. ____________ edendcta

3. After a week of studying for semester tests, on Saturday, Emmalin felt very <u>lethargic</u> and just wanted to relax. ____________ gdlainu

4. Some classic <u>seafaring</u> poems are Samuel Taylor Coleridge's "The Rime of the Ancient Mariner," and John Masefield's "Sea Fever." ____________ eimmtari

5. Ms. Palmer emphasized that it was wrong to be <u>stubborn</u> in opinions, refusing to at least listen to those with contradictory arguments. ____________ aeoibstnt

6. The suggestion that the world was round was a <u>revolutionary</u> idea in many ancient cultures. ____________ iradcla

7. Kara was very <u>chatty</u> about her trip when she returned from a family visit to Vancouver in British Columbia. ____________ uslogruar

8. A favorite saying of Mr. Collins is, "If you can't say something nice—don't say it," showing how he feels about <u>disparaging</u> comments about others. ____________ aesldruson

9. "Strive to always be <u>coherent</u> in your writing," advised Ms. Paterson to her composition students. ____________ diluc

**E.** Write the word, idiom, or phrase from the choice box that best defines each list word.

- listless
- loquacious
- defamatory
- extreme
- self-indulgent
- nautical
- tongue-in-cheek
- evident
- inflexible
- unctuous

1. slanderous ____________________
2. decadent ____________________
3. facetious ____________________
4. obstinate ____________________
5. lucid ____________________
6. languid ____________________
7. maritime ____________________
8. garrulous ____________________
9. radical ____________________

**F.** Complete each sentence to show that you understand the meaning of the underlined word.

1. "That's <u>slanderous</u>," Hope declared when Mandy said ______________________________
______________________________________________________________________________.

2. "My uncle lives a <u>decadent</u> life because he ______________________________
______________________________________________________________," explained Luke.

3. "I was only being <u>facetious</u>," apologized Kara after she told Suzanne that ______________
______________________________________________________________________________.

4. "My dog Rudy is so <u>obstinate</u> that he ______________________________
________________________________________________________," complained Caroline.

5. "One way to make sure that your writing is <u>lucid</u> is to ______________________________
_______________________________________________________," advised Ms. Paterson.

6. After he ______________________________________________________________
________________________________________ Max had good reason to feel <u>languid</u>.

7. "A perfect title for a collection of <u>maritime</u> short stories might be ____________________
___________________________________________________________________," said Bernie.

8. Gary is <u>garrulous</u> at inappropriate times such as ______________________________
______________________________________________________________________________.

9. The crowd of people gathered together before the Capitol Building in Washington, D.C., displayed <u>radical</u> behavior by ______________________________________________
______________________________________________________________________________.

# Vocabulary List 8
## Adverbs That Begin With the Letter "C"

| **Word**<br>[pronunciation]<br>**other word form** | **Definition**<br>• sample sentence |
|---|---|
|  |  |
| **chauvinistically**<br>[SHOH vuh nist ih kul lee]<br>**chauvinist** (n)<br>**chauvinism** (n) | showing excessive support for one's own cause, group, or gender<br>• She chauvinistically claimed that girls were better at math than boys. |
| **chivalrously**<br>[SHIV uhl rus lee]<br>**chivalry** (n) | behaving in a courteous or gallant way<br>• Chivalrously, he opened the car door for his mom and offered to carry her packages. |
| **circuitously**<br>[sur KYOO ih tuhs lee]<br>**circuitous** (adj) | in a roundabout way rather than in a direct way<br>• Shane circuitously explained why he arrived home two hours after curfew. |
| **clairvoyantly**<br>[klair VOY uhnt lee]<br>**clairvoyant** (adj)<br>**clairvoyance** (n) | having the power of seeing objects or actions beyond the range of natural vision<br>• The fortune-teller claimed that she could clairvoyantly see the future in tea leaves. |
| **coherently**<br>[koh HEER uhnt lee]<br>**coherence** (n) | in a clear, logical way<br>• Rachel coherently supported each of her arguments with proof. |
| **complaisantly**<br>[kuhm PLEY sunt lee] | agreeable and willing to please others<br>• After the students asked him, Mr. Clark complaisantly postponed the social studies quiz until Friday. |
| **conscientiously**<br>[kon shee EN shuhs lee] | controlled by or done according to one's sense of what is right<br>• Becky conscientiously called home whenever she knew she would be late. |
| **curmudgeonly**<br>[ker MUHJ uhn lee]<br>**curmudgeon** (n) | bad tempered or surly<br>• He acts in such a curmudgeonly way that he has few friends. |
| **cynically**<br>[SIN ih kuhl lee]<br>**cynic** (n)<br>**cynicism** (n) | distrustful of human sincerity or integrity<br>• Mom laughed cynically when Dylan said his chores were finished. |

**A.** Write synonyms or antonyms before each pair of words.

1. ______________________________ cynically – trustfully
2. ______________________________ conscientiously – painstakingly
3. ______________________________ circuitously – directly
4. ______________________________ complaisantly – disobediently
5. ______________________________ chauvinistically – prejudicially
6. ______________________________ curmudgeonly – kindly
7. ______________________________ clairvoyantly – perceptively
8. ______________________________ coherently – incomprehensibly
9. ______________________________ chivalrously – politely

**B.** Write the best word from the choice box to complete each sentence.

| | | |
|---|---|---|
| clairvoyant | coherence | circuitous |
| conscientiously | curmudgeon | cynicism |
| chauvinism | cynic | clairvoyance |
| chivalry | chauvinist | |
| copious | complaisantly | |

1. Milly ________________________ practiced each day for her upcoming piano recital.

2. In an unusual display of ____________________________, Luke helped Rachel pick up her books when she accidentally dropped them in the hall.

3. With ________________________, Ms. Paterson explained the steps in the writing process: prewriting, drafting, revising, editing, and publishing.

4. Shane seemed ___________________________ when he predicted victory for the Jefferson Cougar's football team on Saturday.

5. Christina admitted that she acted like a/an _____________________________ when Dylan asked to borrow school supplies because he never returned things.

6. All the girls glared at Luke, declaring that he was acting like a/an ___________________, when he said that a woman should never be elected president.

7. Emmalin _______________________ offered to be a buddy to the new student in the class.

8. Instead of riding his bike directly to Casey's house, Tim took a/an ____________________ route through the park and past Hope's house.

9. Mom, who loved the luxury of staying in a nice hotel on vacation, replied with _________________________ saying, "I can hardly wait," when Dad gleefully announced that the family would be hiking and camping in Big Bear National Park this summer.

10. Displaying ________________________ in a foreign country, such as complaining about everything different, is rude and unfriendly.

11. Just for fun at the annual school fair, Hillary pretended to have ______________________ and used a fake crystal ball to tell futures.

12. A philosopher, known as a/an ________________________ in ancient Greece, rejected social and political practices of the time.

### C. Story Challenge

Write the best word from the choice box to fill each blank in the story.

| | | | |
|---|---|---|---|
| chauvinistically | coherently | curmudgeonly | complaisantly |
| cynically | circuitously | conscientiously | clairvoyantly |
| chivalrously | unethically | | |

## Adverbs Take the Stage

The students in Mr. Stewart's writing class were eager to write a short story. He reviewed the importance of creating believable, interesting characters and to "show, not tell." Mr. Stewart decided to use the week's vocabulary words as the catalyst for a practice writing exercise.

"What I would like you to do today is to portray a fictional character using the methods of characterization that we have discussed. Portray your character by his or her actions, by speaking, thinking, and being spoken about. Use one of the vocabulary words to determine how the character acts, speaks, thinks, and is spoken about, without actually using the vocabulary word."

For example, imagine that my fictional character, Brendan, had the following thought about a friend of his—"I know he's lying," Brendan thought. "He pretends to be my friend, but it's only so he can copy my math homework."

"(1)__________________________, would be the word," said Mandy. "And you used Brendan's thoughts to show that he doesn't trust his friend's motives."

"Good, Mandy. Class, please take about fifteen minutes to think and write, and then I'll ask for your examples," Mr. Stewart instructed.

After the time had elapsed, Julia raised her hand to give her example.

> "Tom noticed the young mother struggling, trying to carry her groceries with one arm and to hold her crying toddler with her other arm. Tom offered to help by carrying her groceries to her car."

"(2)__________________________ is the word, and Julia showed the character Tom in action," said Tim. "May I be next?" he asked. Tim offered his fictional example, explaining that it was two kids talking in science class.

 

> "I like how Ms. Snider carefully explains the process of dissecting the frogs," said Aiden. "To make sure everyone understands, she goes over the steps again and again and then asks if anyone has a question."

"(3)____________________________," said Christopher. "Tim's example shows that the science teacher teaches in a logical way, and we know that from what the two kids say about her."

Christopher was next. "My example also reveals character by what others say," he explained.

> Joe whispered to Brad. "Doesn't she ever smile or have a cheery word for anyone? This is going to be a long year in history class with her as a teacher."

"(4)____________________________ is the word, and Chris showed us that the teacher was rather bad-tempered by having Joe talk about her like Tim did in his example," offered Matt.

"Excellent work," said Mr. Stewart. "Now I will give you some examples and see if you can match the example to the vocabulary word." Mr. Stewart began his examples,

> "Twice he checked his backpack to make sure he had all his homework assignments and the supplies he needed for the day."

"Character in action," said Bernie. "And the vocabulary word is (5)__________________"

Mr. Stewart gave his next example.

> "Sure, I'll help you with your social studies assignment," Lloyd replied when Patrick once again asked for help.

Christina replied—"Character's words," she said. "Lloyd (6)_________________________ replies to Patrick's request."

"Next example," said Mr. Stewart.

> "I know it's going to rain," said Linda. "Every time my nose itches, I know rain is on the way," she said.

Hope replied, "Through her words, we know that Linda thinks (7)__________________. She thinks she can predict the future by how her nose feels."

"Good, Hope. Here's another example."

> "Get to the point!" said Sam's mother. "Just spit it out. Why does it take you forever to admit to punching your brother?"

"Obviously Sam has the habit of speaking (8)______________________________, and we know that through his mother's words," said Shane.

"One more example and we'll be finished for the day," said Mr. Stewart.

> "Men are much better drivers than women," thought the man angrily as he honked his horn at the young woman in the car ahead of him who wasn't going quite as fast as he thought she should."

"First of all, Hiss and Double-Boo," said Suzanne. "This man thinks very (9)____________________________," she said. "He shows that through his very biased thoughts."

"Ok, quiz tomorrow on all the words," Mr. Stewart reminded. "Also, I will include a question about the methods of characterization used by writers."

Some Curmudgeons In Literature

- Ebeneezer Scrooge in *A Christmas Carol*
- Oscar the Grouch from *Sesame Street*
- Severus Snape in the *Harry Potter* books
- Katherina in Shakespeare's *The Taming of the Shrew*
- The Grinch in *How the Grinch Stole Christmas*

 

**D.** The underlined part in each sentence is a synonym, idiom, phrase, or definition for a list word. Unscramble the list word and write the word on the blank.

1. Acting like she had the ability to know the future, Cindy predicted that someday she would be a famous movie actress who would win an Academy Award. ________________ olyatvycranli
2. When the princess was threatened by the fire-breathing dragon, the knight in shining armor gallantly came to her rescue. ________________ olisucvylahr
3. Mandy's job was to take her younger sister Bella to preschool, and she diligently made sure that Bella arrived on time and then walked her to her classroom. ________________ leusictoniycnso
4. The bad-tempered store clerk refused to exchange the sweater that Heidi wanted to return for another color, suggesting that Heidi had already worn the sweater. ________________ nlucymrgdoeu
5. The woman xenophobically refused to be cared for by a male nurse, because she said a man was not capable of being a nurse. ________________ slhicylaiunavict
6. Ms. Paterson glanced skeptically at Luke when he promised he would never turn in another late essay. ________________ lcyiaynlc
7. Bernie agreeably said he would walk a dog and clean up after it if he was allowed to have one. ________________ antplolaycmis
8. The witness to the accident rationally gave the policeman an account of what she had observed. ________________ thncyreloe
9. Ann's father indirectly drove from California to Ohio, going through Texas, to stop and visit his sister, Arlene. ________________ lustrcycioui

**E.** Write the word, idiom, or phrase from the choice box that best defines each list word.

- prejudicially
- gallantly
- gruffly
- carefully
- rambling
- disrespectfully
- psychically
- distrustfully
- good-naturedly
- clearly

1. complaisantly ______________________
2. chivalrously ______________________
3. clairvoyantly ______________________
4. chauvinistically ______________________
5. conscientiously ______________________
6. curmudgeonly ______________________
7. circuitously ______________________
8. coherently ______________________
9. cynically ______________________

**F.** Complete each sentence to show that you understand the meaning of the underlined word.

1. Matthew chivalrously ______________________________

   ______________________________.

2. Before he passed in his science project, Casey conscientiously ______________________________

   ______________________________.

3. Clairvoyantly, Coach Greenberg said that ______________________________

   ______________________________.

4. Because Bernie usually reacted complaisantly, his friends were surprised when he

   ______________________________.

5. Even though Caroline was in shock after the accident, she coherently ______________________________

   ______________________________.

6. After school, Aiden circuitously ______________________________

   ______________________________.

7. The substitute teacher curmudgeonly ______________________________

   ______________________________.

8. Her father cynically responded to Rachel's request for $100 by saying, "______________________________

   ______________________________."

9. Luke chauvinistically defended his opinion that ______________________________

   ______________________________.

# Review: Lists 5-8

**A.** Use the clues to complete the crossword puzzle with vocabulary words, synonyms, or information from the activities.

**Across**

3. Faultless
5. Plague
8. Gallant
9. Approval
10. A pause
11. Banal
13. Lazy
14. A person with a bravado is...

**Down**

1. Slanderous
2. Nomadic
4. Ichthyology species have these
6. One with certitude is...
7. Stubborn
8. A channel
9. Betrothal
12. A garrulous person likes to ...

**B.** Circle the answer which best completes the sentence.

1. The **egalitarian** would believe that
   a. the world is flat.
   b. women are superior to men.
   c. all men are created equal

2. A **clairvoyant** person might discuss
   a. WWII.
   b. the future.
   c. the dinner menu.

3. An antonym for **chauvinistically** is
   a. greedy.
   b. egalitarian.
   c. qualified.

4. **Nebulous** writing might be
   a. coherent.
   b. concise.
   c. confusing.

5. A **curmudgeon** might
   a. attend Harvard.
   b. go fishing on a nice day.
   c. refuse to smile.

6. A **decadent** person would
   a. live in a log cabin in the woods.
   b. reserve the penthouse at the Ritz.
   c. eat Brussels sprouts at every meal.

7. A **stoic** would
   a. pay his taxes.
   b. complain loudly.
   c. accept his fate.

8. **Maritime** rules would concern
   a. boaters.
   b. architects.
   c. physicians.

9. A **demagogue** might be found
   a. studying in the library.
   b. giving a fiery speech.
   c. trying to get a bank loan.

10. The best antonym for **facetious** is
   a. flippant.
   b. joking.
   c. serious.

 

**C.** From the list of fictional book titles, write the best word that might be used in each book.

| | | |
|---|---|---|
| disconcerting | autodidactic | clandestine |
| lucid | circuitously | cynically |
| confer | conscientiously | coherently |
| complaisantly | radical | |

1. ________________________ *Will There Ever Be World Peace?*
2. ________________________ *Infamous Spies of the Twentieth Century*
3. ________________________ *Teach Yourself to Speak French*
4. ________________________ *The 1960s: A Decade of Anxiety*
5. ________________________ *The Power of Self-Discipline*
6. ________________________ *Being Agreeable While Disagreeing*
7. ________________________ *The Round-About Way to Self-Realization*
8. ________________________ *5 Steps to Writing a Clear, Concise Essay*
9. ________________________ *Revolutionary Voices of the Women's Suffrage Movement*
10. ________________________ *Choosing Words Carefully for Understanding*

# Vocabulary List 9
## Vaulting Verbs

| Word [pronunciation] other word form | Definition • sample sentence |
|---|---|
|  |  |
| **alienate** [EY lee uh neyt] **alienation** (n) | to make someone feel isolated, estranged, or excluded<br>• Luke alienated many of his classmates by his rude behavior. |
| **confer** [kun FUHR] **conference** (n) | [1]to grant a title, degree, benefit, or right to someone<br>[2]to discuss or exchange opinions with others<br>• [1]A master's degree in the science of nursing was conferred on Rachel's sister, Sarah.<br>• [2]Principal Zhang conferred with Luke about his negative behavior. |
| **corroborate** [kuh ROB uh reyt] | to make certain or confirm<br>• Elsie was late because her dad had a flat tire, and Piper corroborated her excuse. |
| **deflect** [dih FLEKT] | to cause something to change course or direction<br>• The driver tried to deflect blame for the accident by saying her car's gas pedal stuck. |
| **embody** [em BOD ee] **embodiment** (n) | [1]to represent an abstract idea, quality, or principle in tangible form<br>[2]to include something<br>• [1]Emmalin embodies the spirit of friendliness.<br>• [2]The personal freedoms of American citizens are embodied in the Constitution. |
| **fabricate** [FAB rih keyt] **fabrication** (n) | to invent or make up something usually meant to deceive<br>• The detective discovered that the suspect's alibi was fabricated. |
| **galvanize** [GAL vuh niyz] **galvanization** (n) | to shock or excite someone into taking action<br>• With his speech, Principal Zhang galvanized the student body to take action against bullying. |
| **gesticulate** [je STIK yuh leyt] **gesticulation** (n) | to make hand or arm movements when speaking to emphasize what is being said<br>• Ned wildly gesticulated as he told about the mountain lion that crossed his path while he was jogging. |
| **obliterate** [uh BLIT uh reyt] | to completely destroy something<br>• Caroline's father obliterated her hopes of going to Ft. Lauderdale with her friends for Spring Break. |

**A.** Write the list word that might be included in the news story for each headline.

| | | | |
|---|---|---|---|
| confer | galvanize | fabricate | alienate |
| deflect | embody | gesticulate | obliterate |
| decimate | confer | embody | corroborate |

1. ______________________ "Tornado Destroys Small Oklahoma Town"

2. ______________________ "FBI Finds Information Proving Foreign Hacking"

3. ______________________ "Writer Isabel Allende Receives Doctor of Letters Honorary Degree From Harvard"

4. ______________________ "Frantic Signal for Help Saves the Life of Drowning Child"

5. ______________________ "New Health Care Bill Includes Middle Class Tax Breaks"

6. ______________________ "Suspect's Alibi Proves False"

7. ______________________ "Bullet-Proof Vest Saves Detective's Life"

8. ______________________ "Senator's Thoughtless Comment Turns Off Voters"

9. ______________________ "Protesters Take Action Reacting to Budget Cuts for Health and Human Services"

10. ______________________ "Students Study Citizen's Liberties in the Bill of Rights"

11. ______________________ "Parents Meet to Discuss Proposed New High School"

**B.** Write the best word from the choice box to complete each sentence.

| | | | |
|---|---|---|---|
| embodiment | defer | corroborate | galvanization |
| obliterated | gesticulations | alienation | deflect |
| fabrication | conference | | |

1. The ________________________ of two good friends, Piper and Elsie, prompted Emmalin to help them reconcile their differences.

2. Mrs. Denby had a/an ________________________ with Casey about the recent decline in his grades.

3. As she directed the play *Our Town*, Ms. Palmer reminded the actors that ________________________ must be exaggerated to be seen by the audience.

4. Shane is the ________________________ of an outstanding athlete, with initiative, determination, tough-mindedness, and full commitment to be the best he can be.

5. Because Cindy had a bad habit of ________________________ when telling stories, her friends had a difficult time believing her.

6. The attack on Pearl Harbor in 1941 caused the ________________________ of the U.S. to become involved in WWII.

7. In 79 A.D., Mount Vesuvius erupted and ________________________ the Roman cities of Pompeii, Herculaneum, and other settlements.

8. Police officers often wear multi-threat vests designed to ________________________ weapons such as bullets and knives.

9. The defense attorney failed to find a witness to ________________________ the alibi of his client.

**C. Story Challenge**

Write the best word from the choice box to fill each blank in the story.

| confer | justify | galvanize | conferred |
|---|---|---|---|
| obliterate | corroborated | embodies | embody |
| alienate | fabricating | gesticulated | deflect |

## And Then Came the Euphemism

"Ms. Paterson, we had to write jargon poems," said Julia as she entered her writing class. "Do you want to hear mine?" she anxiously inquired.

"Definitely Julia, you know how I like poetry," Ms. Paterson replied. "Furthermore, Mr. Riley (1)____________________________ what you said. He explained about the poetry assignment and said how anxious he was to hear the jargon poems today."

Julia began reading her poem:

**Tempo of My Life**

by Julia Belysheva

A crescendo brings life up high
with a trip to see a movie with a friend
or receive an A on a test
But not for long
Sliding down into the inevitable diminuendo
With loads of homework and music practice
Then my days become
ordinary and mundane
I grumble through Monday
Tuesday and Wednesday are all polyphony
of lecture upon lecture
Thursday and Friday are a series of staccatos
Then after the cadenza of Saturday & Sunday
Monday arrives again
Back to Da Capo al Fine.

"Your poem definitely (2)____________________________ piano jargon," complimented Ms. Paterson. "I recognize all of your terms, except for 'Da Capo al Fine.' What does that mean?" asked Ms. Paterson.

"It means to repeat from the beginning," explained Julia.

To (3)____________________________ her students' attention from the jargon poems they had composed so that she could begin today's lesson, Ms. Paterson (4)____________________________ with a motion of her hand for them to sit down and be silent.

"When Mandy came into the room today, she asked me if she could please use the restroom," began Ms. Paterson. "Mandy was using a euphemism," she explained. "<u>A euphemism is a polite, indirect expression which replaces a word or a phrase that might be considered harsh, impolite, or unpleasant</u>."

"I have an example," said Luke. "Yesterday, Principal Zhang said he wanted to (5)____________________________ with a friend of mine about (6)____________________________ the truth, when Principal Zhang really planned to discipline him for lying by forging his dad's signature on an excuse note."

"Good," said Ms. Paterson. "Can anyone else give an example?"

"In history class, we learned that during the period of WWII, Hitler was guilty of ethnic cleansing—definitely a softer expression than what he really did—try to (7)____________________________ a whole race of people by murdering them," offered Aiden.

"I have an example," offered Ned. "My aunt is a social worker who works with young adults who have been in trouble with the law. To (8)____________________________ their thoughts about the consequences of breaking the law when they become adults, Aunt Claire took a group to visit a correctional facility—a euphemism for prison."

"My neighbor," began Harvey, "said a title was (9)____________________________ on her son when he started a new job. The title was Sanitary Engineer, which is really a euphemism for garbage collector."

"Yes, that would be a euphemism," said Ms. Paterson. "How many of you have read the novel *Animal Farm* by George Orwell?" she asked, and many students raised their hands. "The words of Squealer, a character in the story, (10)____________________________ a euphemism when he explains that the farm animals will get less food. Squealer deliberately softens the news when he says, 'For the time being, it has been found necessary to make a readjustment of rations.'"

"One more example, and we'll end class for today," said Ms. Paterson. "Politicians are notorious for using euphemisms, so they do not [11]____________________________ the voting public. For example, instead of saying poor people, they might say economically disadvantaged. Or instead of using the word slums, they might say substandard housing. Have a great day, and be on the alert for euphemisms," Ms. Paterson concluded as class ended.

Common Euphemisms

- a little thin on top (balding)
- be excused (use the bathroom)
- economical with the truth (lying)
- between jobs (unemployed)
- couch potato (lazy person)
- senior citizen (old person)
- the birds and the bees (sex)

 

**D.** The underlined part in each sentence is a synonym, idiom, phrase, or definition for a list word. Unscramble the list word and write the word on the blank.

1. In 2005, Hurricane Katrina thundered onto the Gulf Coast <u>destroying</u> property and taking lives. ____________ gaieontbrilt

2. From her seat in the bleachers, Milly <u>used hand and arm motions</u> to signal to her friends who entered the gymnasium. ____________ eiugtelsdcat

3. In his debate, Tim <u>supported</u> his arguments that the voting age should be lowered with logical facts and opinions from experts. ____________ ebdrocootrra

4. Casey was <u>shocked</u> into putting more time on his essay assignments when he received a D on his last paper. ____________ zaiegvndal

5. In fencing, the term "parry" means to <u>divert</u> a thrust or blow by an opponent. ____________ ledtefc

6. In his morning announcements, Principal Zhang complimented Mrs. Bradley, who had an important honor <u>bestowed</u> on her by becoming the first runner-up to national teacher of the year. ____________ enrcoedfr

7. Mrs. Bradley was chosen because she <u>represented</u> the qualities of an excellent teacher—good classroom management skills, an engaging teaching style, and having high expectations for her students. ____________ iomedbed

8. Mr. Clark <u>consulted</u> with Principal Zhang before planning a trip for his history class to go to Boston, Massachusetts. ____________ fcrdoeern

9. In Shakespeare's *Romeo and Juliet*, the Montague family was <u>estranged</u> from the Capulet family. ____________ ladineeta

10. The man was stopped by security at the airport when it was discovered that he had a counterfeit passport with information that had been <u>falsified</u>. ____________ bcdarfetia

11. The school handbook <u>included</u> such things as school rules, an academic calendar, and a list of current administration and faculty members. ____________ mdbedioe

**E.** Write the word, idiom, or phrase from the choice box that best defines each list word.

- destroy
- motion (v)
- validate
- inspire
- divert
- consult
- enthusiastic
- award to
- represent
- turn away
- falsify
- integrate

1. embody ______________________
2. confer ______________________
3. deflect ______________________
4. embody ______________________
5. gesticulate ______________________
6. alienate ______________________
7. confer ______________________
8. obliterate ______________________
9. corroborate ______________________
10. fabricate ______________________
11. galvanize ______________________

**F.** Complete each sentence to show that you understand the meaning of the underlined word.

1. Heidi embodies school spirit by ______________________________

______________________________.

2. During his wrestling match, Christopher deflected getting pinned by his opponent when he

______________________________.

3. Mrs. Denby, the music teacher, conferred with John about ______________________________

______________________________.

4. Piper gesticulated as she gave her speech about taekwondo by ______________________________

______________________________.

5. The American Declaration of Independence embodies the idea that ______________________________

______________________________.

6. Hope and Elsie, who were once good friends, became alienated from each other when

______________________________.

7. At the end of the year Honor's Assembly, Principal Zhang conferred ______________________________

______________________________.

8. "Did you fabricate that story?" Mr. Stewart asked when Dylan ______________________________

______________________________.

9. Ms. Palmer stressed to her journalism class that it was always important to corroborate

______________________________.

10. At half time, Coach Greenberg tried to galvanize the basketball team by ______________________________

______________________________.

11. In the dystopian novel that Mandy was reading, Earth had been obliterated by ______________________________

______________________________.

# Vocabulary List 10
## Amazing Adjectives

| **Word**<br>[pronunciation]<br>**other word form** | **Definition**<br>• sample sentence |
|---|---|
|  |  |
| **arbitrary**<br>[AHR bih trer ee]<br>**arbitrariness** (n) | subject to individual judgment or personal whim<br>• Ms. Palmer gave her students an arbitrary choice of topics for a three-minute speech. |
| **condescending**<br>[kon duh SEN ding]<br>**condescension** (n) | showing a superior attitude toward others<br>• Sometimes older brothers and sisters act in a condescending way to their younger siblings. |
| **culpable**<br>[KUHL puh buhl]<br>**culpability** (n) | deserving blame<br>• Casey was culpable of leaving the door unlocked when he left for school in the morning. |
| **gratuitous**<br>[gruh TOO ih tuhs]<br>**gratuity** (n) | [1]given or received free of charge [2]uncalled for or unnecessary<br>• [1]Parking and luggage handling were gratuitous at the hotel.<br>• [2]The movie didn't need the gratuitous violence. |
| **incisive**<br>[in SAHY siv]<br>**incisiveness** (n)<br>**incision** (n) | remarkably clear and direct<br>• "With her incisive answer of 'No way,' I knew Mom wouldn't let me go to Florida for spring break with my friend," said Julia. |
| **prehensile**<br>[pree HEN siyl]<br>**prehensility** (n) | adapted for seizing, grasping, or taking hold of something<br>• Opossums have prehensile tails. |
| **retrospective**<br>[re truh SPEK tiv]<br>**retrospection** (n) | looking back at the past<br>• Dad took a retrospective look at his old high school yearbooks. |
| **unanimous**<br>[yoo NAN uh muhs]<br>**unanimity** (n) | in complete agreement<br>• The opinion was unanimous that a quality of a good friendship is mutual respect. |
| **unctuous**<br>[UHK choo uhs] | excessively smooth, suave, or smug<br>• A person who acts in an unctuous way usually wants something from you. |

**A.** Write the best list word that the synonyms, idioms, or phrases define to complete each sentence.

| condescending | stoic | prehensile | retrospective |
|---|---|---|---|
| arbitrary | gratuitous | unanimous | unctuous |
| culpable | incisive | gratuitous | |

1. The ______________________________ politician shook hands, kissed babies, and sampled the homemade cookies hoping he could generate some votes.

   slick ingratiating fawning insincere

2. "Mandy is sometimes so ______________________________ in our group discussions," said Hope. "She acts like she's the only one with the right opinion."

   patronizing arrogant stuck-up lordly

3. In his debate defending censorship, Bernie cited examples of films and video games that contained ______________________________ violence.

   unnecessary needless unjustified uncalled for

4. Chameleons can wrap their ______________________________ tails around branches while climbing trees.

   seizing grasping gripping taking hold

5. The presiding judge declared a mistrial after the jury failed to reach an ________________________ verdict.

   uncontested unified as one in accord

6. Ned felt ______________________________ because he missed the free throw shot that would have won the basketball game.

   guilty at fault responsible liable

7. In gym class, Ms. Cosgrove used a/an ______________________________ method to choose teams for volleyball by pulling names from a box.

   random by chance capricious erratic

8. People often take a/an ______________________________ look at the last year on New Year's Eve.

   reflective contemplative reminiscent nostalgic

9. The food critic for the local newspaper wrote a/an ______________________________ article finding fault with not only the food, but the service at the new restaurant.

   keen penetrating acute concise

10. At Comic Con, the annual pop-culture convention in San Diego, T-shirts and souvenir books were ______________________________ to the first 100 attendees.

    complimentary on the house gratis without charge

**B.** Write the best word from the choice box to complete each sentence.

| | | | |
|---|---|---|---|
| arbitrariness | retrospection | gratuity | unctuous |
| incisiveness | condescension | prehensility | incision |
| clandestine | culpability | unanimity | |

1. One of Ms. Paterson's journal prompts suggested that each student use ________________________ and take a look at their younger years and then write about growth in wisdom—what has been learned about life, about self, and about others.

2. Piper's brother Charlie had chocolate on his mouth, so it seems he has some ________________________ for eating the last piece of her birthday cake.

3. ________________________ is a characteristic of some reptiles such as chameleons and geckos, and some fish such as seahorses and pipefish.

4. The ________________________ of the vote showed complete support for a field trip to the local aquarium.

5. The ________________________ of weekday mealtimes at Ned's house is determined by the different work and school schedules of family members.

6. Danny, Dylan's older brother, was guilty of ________________________ by the way he treated Danny—acting as though he had the answers to everything.

7. The ________________________ of Mrs. Bradley's decision made it obvious that she would not accept late science projects.

8. The ________________________ of the doctors involved in "Doctors Without Borders" is appreciated because these doctors and other members of the medical profession donate their services to those in need throughout the world.

9. Mr. Clark spoke with ________________________ about his expectations in history class, leaving no doubt about the requirements to pass his class.

10. "Others can usually recognize ________________________ behavior," reminded Principal Zhang. "So remember to always be authentic and sincere with compliments."

## C. Story Challenge

Write the best word from the choice box to fill each blank in the story.

| | | | |
|---|---|---|---|
| arbitrary | lucid | prehensile | unctuous |
| condescending | gratuitous | unanimous | gratuitous |
| culpable | incisive | retrospective | |

### Advice From Ben Franklin

In Mrs. Cole's class, the students were studying the history and literature of the period from 1600 to 1800. Currently, they were learning about multi-talented Benjamin Franklin. The focus today was on Franklin's writings in *The Autobiography* and *Poor Richard's Almanac*.

In *The Autobiography*, Benjamin Franklin showed 18th century ideals of reason, order, and human perfectibility. He thought it was possible to achieve moral perfection and listed and explained the thirteen virtues that he thought were necessary to achieve this perfection: temperance, silence, order, resolution, frugality, industry, sincerity, justice, moderation, cleanliness, tranquility, chastity, and humility.

On the other hand, Franklin's *Poor Richard's Almanac* was a calendar filled with weather forecasts, recipes, jokes, and witty sayings called aphorisms. Mrs. Cole liked to connect the week's vocabulary words to one of her lessons. Today, she asked her class to connect a vocabulary word to a quotation or an aphorism of Benjamin Franklin and to explain it to the class.

After the class had time to check the Internet as well as other resources in the room, the students were ready to respond. Casey volunteered to be first. "I chose the word (1)________________________," he explained. "When Franklin says, 'Honesty is the best policy,' I think he includes the idea that it's wrong to flatter people unless you really mean what you say."

Hillary was next. "(2)________________________ is the word I chose. That word reminds me of Franklin's words, 'Blessed is he that expects nothing, for he shall never be disappointed.' I think Franklin means that we shouldn't expect things to be given to us freely and that we should be prepared to work for what we want."

"Interesting interpretation, Hillary," said Mrs. Cole.

Shane volunteered. "My word is (3)______________________________ and Benjamin Franklin says, 'Whatever is begun in anger ends in shame.' Maybe he means that if you use angry words or actions, you feel guilty and embarrassed afterwards."

"Very perceptive, Shane," said Mrs. Cole.

Kara volunteered to be next. "(4)______________________________ is the word I chose," said Kara. "I think that the Franklin aphorism that connects to the word is 'Humility makes great men twice honorable,'" she said. "People usually admire those who don't brag about their accomplishments and go around acting like they're superior to others," Kara explained.

"Good, Kara. Milly you seem eager to give your example."

"My Franklin quote is this," Milly offered. 'One today is worth two tomorrows.' That quote reminds me of the word (5)______________________________. I think Franklin is saying not to worry looking back over past mistakes, but to do something positive in the present."

"I like all of your personal interpretations," Mrs. Cole complimented. Aiden volunteered to be next.

"Ms. Paterson always reminds us not to think that an abundance of words makes an essay better," said Aiden. "So when Franklin says, 'He that speaks much is much mistaken,' I think of the word (6)______________________________, which to me means being clear and concise in what you say or write."

"I'll let Ms. Paterson know that you remembered her writing advice," said Mrs. Cole. "Shall we continue with examples?" she asked.

The vote was (7)______________________________. Every student had an example and wanted to read it to the class.

Max had his hand up. "This may be a bit weird, but I chose the word (8)______________________________ and the idea of not trying to seize or grab more than you need. And the Franklin quote is this: 'If you be wealthy, think of saving as well as getting.'"

"Not weird at all," said Mrs. Cole. "I'd say that's a creative interpretation."

"Mine is a bit of a stretch too," said Bernie. "But to me, the word (9)______________________________ could mean that a person acts according to his or her own whim or wishes, without asking for advice. When Franklin says, 'A man wrapped up in himself makes a very small bundle,' I think he's saying that asking for advice or input from others can be a good thing."

Students continued giving creative examples until the bell rang and class ended. "You all amaze me," said Mrs. Cole. "I think I have a bevy of philosophers in this class. Furthermore, no (10)______________________________ silly comments were given. Each of your examples was relevant to Ben Franklin and his wise words. Remember, you have a quiz tomorrow and as Franklin said, 'By failing to prepare, you are preparing to fail.'"

More Franklin Aphorisms

- There are no gains without pains.
- The noblest question in the world is "What good may I do in it?"
- He that lies down with dogs shall rise up with fleas.
- Beware of little expenses, a small leak will sink a great ship.
- No better relation than a prudent and faithful friend.

 

**D.** The underlined part in each sentence is a synonym, idiom, phrase, or definition for a list word. Unscramble the list word and write the word on the blank.

1. Ms. Palmer placed a random selection of topics on slips of paper in a box, and without looking, each student had to draw a slip of paper and give a two-minute speech on the topic. ________________ ariayrbtr

2. The restaurant paid minimum wages to its waiters and waitresses but complimentary tips were usually quite generous. ________________ utasgturio

3. Some believe that water pollution is responsible for coral reef destruction. ________________ leupbalc

4. We appreciated the movie critic's brief, but clear critiques. ________________ ceivisin

5. The elephant uses its grasping trunk to forage for food. ________________ esreihnelp

6. Many historians and scholars are in agreement that Leonardo da Vinci is the perfect example of a Renaissance man. ________________ asminunou

7. "Gifts and insincere compliments will not help your grade," teased Mr. Clark. "However, good note-taking, study, and class participation will serve you well." ________________ utnsoucu

8. "My dad has a superior attitude and always criticizes whatever I do," complained Michael. ________________ nedcngodeicsn

9. Everyone gave Luke a dirty look when he made an unnecessary unkind comment about Celeste's new hair style. ________________ outigutras

10. Ms. Paterson asked her writing students to take a reflective look at the past and write a narrative essay about a childhood event. ________________ eitprevotsrec

**E.** Write the word, idiom, or phrase from the choice box that best defines each list word.

- unpredictable
- superiority
- blameworthy
- free
- unnecessary
- able to grasp
- sharp
- all in accord
- reminiscent
- sneaky
- insincere
- flattery

1. retrospective ____________________

2. unanimous ____________________

3. gratuitous ____________________

4. condescending ____________________

5. prehensile ____________________

6. culpable ____________________

7. unctuous ____________________

8. incisive ____________________

9. gratuitous ____________________

10. arbitrary ____________________

**F.** Complete each sentence to show that you understand the meaning of the underlined word.

1. Kelly has an <u>unctuous</u> habit of ______________________________________________

    ________________________________________________________________________.

2. Dylan's <u>arbitrary</u> ideas for a demonstration speech included ______________________

    ________________________________________________________________________.

3. With its <u>prehensile</u> tail, the ___________________________ could _________________

    ________________________________________________________________________.

4. "My dad was in a <u>retrospective</u> mood and he ____________________________________

    ________________________________________________________," mused Gary.

5. On vacation, Bernie and his family enjoyed the <u>gratuitous</u> perks offered by the hotel such as

    ________________________________________________________________________.

6. Luke was <u>culpable</u> of ______________________________________________________

    ________________________________________________________________________

7. The class would probably be <u>unanimous</u> about _________________________________

    ________________________________________________________________________

8. "I liked the book," said Ned, "but the ____________________________________________

    ______________________________________________________ seemed <u>gratuitous</u>."

9. "Ms. Paterson jots <u>incisive</u> comments on our essays such as _______________________

    ________________________________________________________," said Rachel.

10. "My sister Lucy is so <u>condescending</u>, she always _________________________________

    __________________________________________________," complained Hannah.

# Vocabulary List 11
## Necessary Nouns

| **Word**<br>[pronunciation]<br>**other word form**<br> | **Definition**<br>• sample sentence<br> |
|---|---|
| **gastronomy**<br>[ga STRON uh mee]<br>**gastronomical** (adj) | the art and practice of choosing, cooking, and eating good food<br>• The chef took classes in gastronomy at Le Cordon Bleu in Paris, France. |
| **genealogy**<br>[jee nee OL uh jee] | the study of family history using historical documents, DNA samples, or other available resources<br>• Shane's mother explored the genealogy of his family using historical documents. |
| **idiosyncrasy**<br>[id ee uh SING kruh see]<br>**idiosyncratic** (adj) | a characteristic, habit, or mannerism that is unique to an individual<br>• One of Gary's idiosyncrasies is to use his hands when he speaks. |
| **manifesto**<br>[man uh FES toh] | a public declaration of the policy and aims of a group or organization<br>• The U.S. Declaration of Independence is a manifesto that was considered an act of treason against England when it was written. |
| **obscurity**<br>[ohb SKUR ih tee]<br>**obscure** (adj) | being unknown, inconspicuous, or unimportant<br>• The typewriter faded into obscurity when computers became widely used. |
| **obsolescence**<br>[ob suh LES uhns]<br>**obsolete** (n) | no longer produced or used; out of date<br>• The use of salt to preserve food faded into obsolescence when refrigeration was invented. |
| **pathos**<br>[PEY thohs] | an emotional appeal, such as anger or pity, used in persuasion<br>• The movie *Beaches* is filled with pathos. |
| **quandary**<br>[KWON duh ree] | uncertainty about what to do in a difficult situation<br>• Heidi was in a quandary about finding a paying summer job or working as a volunteer at an animal rescue center. |
| **treason**<br>[TREE zuhn]<br>**treasonous** (adj) | the crime of betraying one's country by helping an enemy or trying to destroy the country's government<br>• One of America's most notorious persons convicted of treason was Benedict Arnold. |

**A.** Write the best list word that the synonyms, idioms, or phrases define to complete each sentence.

| | | | |
|---|---|---|---|
| genealogy | manifesto | obsolescence | treason |
| quandary | obscurity | pathos | discord |
| idiosyncrasy | gastronomy | | |

1. Edgar Allan Poe lived in ______________________________, but after his death in 1849, he was celebrated as the most important detective novelist of all time.

   anonymity oblivion insignificance unknown

2. John has the _________________________ of putting hot mustard on his scrambled eggs.

   mannerism peculiarity eccentricity quirk

3. Hannah's mother framed and hung a family ____________________________ tree, complete with illustrative photographs, in the living room.

   ancestry pedigree lineage genetics

4. In Frank Stockton's short story "The Lady, or the Tiger," the protagonist has a/an ________________________________ that involves making a difficult choice.

   dilemma predicament plight perplexity

5. John's mother told him that the gimmicky fad that was popular when she was in high school and has since fell into ________________________________ was the pet rock.

   elimination discontinued use destruction thing of the past

6. The International Academy of _________________________________ is in Paris, France, where the preparation of food is serious business.

   cuisine cooking culinary science food

7. American presidents can be impeached for _____________________________, bribery, or other high crimes and misdemeanors.

   sedition duplicity subversion breach of faith

8. Brendan posted a/an _________________________________ in the school newspaper listing all the reasons why he should be elected Student Council president.

   public notice platform proclamation announcement

9. Eponine's solo "On My Own," from the musical *Les Miserables* is filled with ________________________________.

   poignancy emotion sentiment passion

**B.** Write the best word from the choice box to complete each sentence.

| | | | |
|---|---|---|---|
| quandary | hiatus | idiosyncratic | genealogy |
| obscure | gastronomical | obsolete | manifesto |
| pathos | treasonous | | |

1. In the 1600s, when Guy Fawkes tried to assassinate King James I of England, he was convicted of ______________________________ actions and sentenced to death.

2. In Homer's *Odyssey*, Odysseus and his men face a ______________________________ when they find themselves trapped in the cave of the murderous Cyclops.

3. Some fear that the American factory worker will become ______________________________ because of the use of robots.

4. YouTube videos are responsible for some musicians to rise from being ______________________________ to becoming famous.

5. Tim used ______________________________ in his persuasive speech by arousing anger in his audience about Africa's children whose growth is stunted because of lack of nutritious food.

6. For her birthday, Ann received an ancestry ______________________________ kit that uses a small saliva sample to analyze DNA to find her personal ethnic roots.

7. Many people consider Martin Luther King's famous "I Have a Dream" speech, delivered in 1963, to be a famous ______________________________ in American history.

8. In Speech class, Ms. Palmer advised her students to avoid the annoying ______________________________ habit of saying "um," continually during a speech.

9. "To me, ______________________________ delights mean beef jerky and barbeque chips," joked Harvey.

### C. Story Challenge

Write the best word from the choice box to fill each blank in the story.

| | | | |
|---|---|---|---|
| pathos | treason | gastronomy | obsolescence |
| genealogy | idiosyncrasy | quandary | obscurity |
| pandemic | manifesto | | |

## The Renaissance Rebirth

"Harvey, are you ready for the test on the Renaissance today?" teased Mr. Clark. Mr. Riley tells me you were reviewing Renaissance jargon in writing class for the test."

"I'm in a definite (1) ____________________________ if you're serious," said Harvey.

"The Renaissance period remains in (2) ____________________________ for me until I know more about it," he confessed.

"Good place to begin," said Mr. Clark. "The word renaissance means 'rebirth.' Historians use the term to describe the period from approximately the 15th through the early 17th centuries. No (3) ____________________________ exists that states the goals or the aims of this period in European history, but definite changes occurred. The Middle Ages—from the Fall of Rome in 476 A.D. to the 14th century—were seen by many as a time when the emphasis was on the next world. People were more concerned, in a religious sense, with life after death. The individual's life on Earth was of much less importance."

Mr. Clark continued, "During the Renaissance, Italians such as Petrarch and Boccaccio began tracking down and rediscovering classical manuscripts from Greece and Rome that were in (4) ____________________________. These men, called humanists, who studied these revived manuscripts, believed that they came from a period of rationality and logic that had faded during the Middle Ages. The humanists believed that human excellence was important in this world and not only as a qualification to enter a world after death."

"Additionally," explained Mr. Clark, "The humanists wished to revive the languages of ancient Greece and Rome, as well as the values and the intellectual and artistic traditions of these ancient civilizations. Instead of religious subjects, histories began to focus on secular subjects such as politics, war, and diplomacy. An example would be *The Prince*, a book of political philosophy, written by Niccolo Machiavelli."

"Also during the Renaissance period," Mr. Clark continued, "two of the most important inventions appeared—gunpowder brought to Europe by travelers from Asia and the printing press—which made the dissemination of information much faster."

"Furthermore," explained Mr. Clark, "a new scientific spirit developed. Before the Renaissance, people thought the study of religion was the most important branch of learning, and often superstition replaced science in ways of thinking; but during the Renaissance, medicine and other sciences took on a new importance. In fact, during this period the beginnings of modern research occurred with men such as William Harvey, who explained blood circulation and Anton van Leeuwenhoek, who first observed bacteria under a microscope."

Heidi raised her hand and said her mother had completed a/an (5)______________________________ study of her family and found out that her ancestors were from Delft in the Netherlands and that van Leeuwenhoek was a very distant relative.

"That's better than my ancestors," said Luke. "My dad found out that his distant cousin was Benedict Arnold, who was guilty of (6)______________________________ during the American Revolutionary War period."

"Back to the Renaissance," reminded Mr. Clark. "Even music changed. The Italian madrigal, which was a song written to be sung by several voices without instrumental accompaniment, was not a/an (7)______________________________, common only to Italy, but instead spread to England and other European countries. Furthermore, most madrigals had secular themes such as romance, nature, or mythology."

"I know Ms. Steinman plans to discuss Renaissance art in her class this week, and you will see that one of the changes in depicting humans was (8) ______________________________. Artists such as Masaccio portrayed emotions such as sadness or anguish in the faces of his subjects."

It was time for lunch and Mr. Clark announced that because many classes were studying the Renaissance, Mrs. Cummings, the cafeteria supervisor, who had expertise in (9)______________________________ liked to occasionally coordinate her menu with what the students were studying. For today's lunch, she prepared a variety of pasta dishes, an assortment of Italian cheeses, and spumoni for dessert.

### Famous People of the Renaissance

- William Shakespeare
- Machiavelli
- Queen Elizabeth I
- Johannes Gutenberg
- Nicolaus Copernicus
- Marco Polo
- Galileo
- Martin Luther

**D.** The underlined part in each sentence is a synonym, idiom, phrase, or definition for a list word. Unscramble the list word and write the word on the blank.

1. The discontinued use of devices such as cassette tapes is unavoidable as new ways to transmit audio content are discovered.

    ____________________ neeoscbesolc

2. Gary's brother used all the emotion that he could muster in his appeal to his dad to allow him to use the family car to drive to a concert.

    ____________________ ohpsat

3. Milly was frustrated by her uncertainty about whether to research Renaissance music or Renaissance poetry for her essay.

    ____________________ rnyqauad

4. Shane has the peculiarity of wearing the same gray shirt on important test days, declaring that it is his "good luck" shirt.

    ____________________ csyoayidsnir

5. Judas Iscariot was guilty of betrayal when he sold Jesus to Roman soldiers for thirty pieces of silver.

    ____________________ atneors

6. Andre Breton's Surrealist proclamation in 1924 declared that Sigmund Freud's work on dream analysis, free association, and the unconscious were important to imagination and creative expression.

    ____________________ fmoitsaen

7. Mrs. Cummings, the cafeteria supervisor, considered cuisine very important and chose foods that were both healthy and tasty to serve to Jefferson students.

    ____________________ aoyngsmrot

8. To discover information about his family history, Mr. Salter began by purchasing a DNA testing kit.

    ____________________ aeygegoln

9. Because William Shakespeare's plays have universal themes relevant to people in all ages, it is unlikely that he will ever fade into oblivion.

    ____________________ uoycbtirs

**E.** Write the word, idiom, or phrase from the choice box that best defines each list word.

- predicament
- culinary science
- demagogue
- eccentricity
- ancestry
- emotion
- oblivion
- sedition
- thing of the past
- proclamation

1. manifesto ____________________
2. pathos ____________________
3. obscurity ____________________
4. quandary ____________________
5. obsolescence ____________________
6. treason ____________________
7. idiosyncrasy ____________________
8. genealogy ____________________
9. gastronomy ____________________

**F.** Complete each sentence to show that you understand the meaning of the underlined word.

1. Mrs. Bradley, one of the science teachers, passed out a manifesto on the first day of class that stated ______________________________.

2. "What a quandary," said Julia when she realized that ______________________________ ______________________________.

3. An idiosyncrasy of Mrs. Denby, the music teacher, is ______________________________ ______________________________.

4. Bernie used pathos in his persuasive speech about expanding background checks on all gun purchases by ______________________________.

5. An example of an act of treason by a government official might be ______________________________ ______________________________.

6. Mrs. Berkabile, the librarian, purchased some books about gastronomy for the library, and one of the titles was ______________________________.

7. Much to his surprise, when Dylan was doing a genealogy search on his family, he discovered that ______________________________.

8. In response to a journal prompt, Rachel wrote that in 100 years from now she believed that the following three devices will have disappeared into obscurity: ______________________________ ______________________________.

9. The thing that John's grandfather fondly recalls from the past that he wishes had not faded into obsolescence is the ______________________________.

 

# Vocabulary List 12
## Articulate Adjectives

| **Word**<br>[pronunciation]<br>**other word form**<br> | **Definition**<br>• sample sentence<br> |
|---|---|
| **cognizant**<br>[KOG nuh zuhnt] | having knowledge, awareness, or understanding<br>• Principal Zhang made sure that incoming students were <u>cognizant</u> of school rules. |
| **humane**<br>[hyoo MEYN] | characterized by compassion and sympathy for distressed people and animals<br>• The animal shelter provided <u>humane</u> care for all animals in its care. |
| **iconic**<br>[ahy KON ik] | well-known as a representative of a particular idea<br>• *Star Wars* is an <u>iconic</u> example of a modern science fiction movie. |
| **inchoate**<br>[in KOH it] | not yet completed or fully developed<br>• Ms. Steinman said Max had natural and <u>inchoate</u> talent in art. |
| **ludicrous**<br>[LOO di kruhs] | laughable because of obvious absurdity<br>• The claim that the U.S. President was not a citizen was <u>ludicrous</u>. |
| **objective**<br>[uhb JEK tiv] | [1]presenting facts without personal feelings, prejudices, or interpretations [2]a goal or an aim<br>• [1]A good reporter is <u>objective</u>.<br>• [2]Mr. Collin's <u>objective</u> as counselor was to have a meeting with each junior to discuss college. |
| **omniscient**<br>[om NISH uhnt] | having complete or unlimited knowledge, awareness, or understanding<br>• "Aiden seems to think he's <u>omniscient</u> when it comes to history," complained Bernie. |
| **palpable**<br>[PAL pah buhl] | able to be touched or felt<br>• The fear in the movie theater during the horror movie was almost <u>palpable</u>. |
| **quiescent**<br>[kwee ES uhnt] | a state or period of inactivity or repose<br>• "I enjoy just being <u>quiescent</u> on Sunday mornings," said Mandy. |

**A.** Write the best list word that the synonyms, idioms, or phrases define to complete each sentence.

| | | | |
|---|---|---|---|
| cognizant | inchoate | palpable | ludicrous |
| humane | objective | quiescent | objective |
| iconic | omniscient | lucid | |

1. The judge recused herself from the case because as sister-in-law of the defendant, some would question her ability to be __________________________.

   unbiased open-minded equitable impartial

2. The Renaissance painter Caravaggio used dramatic light and shadows to create a __________________________ sense of depth as well as physical and emotional realism.

   clear obvious discernible evident

3. Mozart's __________________________ talent in music was obvious at age six when he was hailed as a wonder child because of his excellent piano playing and improvisations.

   embryonic beginning undeveloped incipient

4. Mauna Kea, on the island of Hawaii, is a/an __________________________ volcano that last erupted in 2460 B.C.

   dormant fallow inactive inert

5. Miles Davis, an American trumpeter, is regarded by many as the ______________________ jazz musician of the 20th century.

   prototypical exemplary paradigmatic archetypical

6. Because of the danger of wildfires in their rural area, Matthew's grandparents were __________________________ of weather reports and warnings.

   aware informed conscious observant

7. The idea that many diseases were caused by microorganisms called germs was first proposed in 1546 and at that time the theory was considered __________________________.

   ridiculous foolish nonsensical preposterous

 

8. In medical school, Rachel's sister Sarah learned that a doctor must not only be proficient, but also ____________________________—capable of compassion.

kind merciful benevolent sympathetic

9. "Mr. Salter must be ____________________________ or have eyes in the back of his head," complained Cindy when Mr. Salter took the note that she was about to hand to Hope.

infinitely wise all-knowing unlimited awareness all-seeing

10. The ____________________________ of the Saturday car wash was to earn enough money for new uniforms for the soccer team.

aim intention purpose goal

**B.** Write the best word from the choice box to complete each sentence.

| | | | |
|---|---|---|---|
| ludicrous | cognizant | omniscient | palpable |
| quiescent | humane | objective | objective |
| gratuitous | iconic | inchoate | |

1. Kara, interested in trying out for the swim team, consulted Emmalin, who was ______________________ of the time demands for practices and swim meets.

2. "My research paper about an important person from the Renaissance period is in its ______________________ stage," said Heidi. "So far, I've only decided to write about Isabella d'Este."

3. John Wayne, one of the most popular film actors of the 20th century, was a/an ______________________ star of Western movies.

4. Some think the idea of Unidentified Flying Objects (UFO's) is ______________________, but others are convinced of their existence.

5. Mrs. Cole explained that a method fiction writers use is the third-person ______________________ point of view, in which the narrator knows the thoughts and feelings of all the characters in the story.

6. Brendan's doctor prescribed ______________________ behavior following his appendectomy surgery until his incision healed.

7. Her friends relied on Rachel for advice because she was a good listener and could be ______________________.

8. Hannah felt a/an ______________________ sense of panic, with sweaty hands and an upset stomach, as she stood in line for the Millennium Force Roller Coaster.

9. Ms. Palmer's primary ______________________ was to ensure that each student in her speech class learned to be a confident speaker.

10. Father Joe's Village in San Diego provides ______________________ and considerate care for the unfortunate.

 

## C. Story Challenge

Write the best word from the choice box to fill each blank in the story.

| | | | |
|---|---|---|---|
| palpable | omniscient | condescending | quiescent |
| inchoate | iconic | cognizant | ludicrous |
| objective | humane | objective | |

### An Architect, a Sculptor, and a Painter

"You all may begin to feel as though the Renaissance is (1)___________________________," joked Ms. Steinman as the students entered art class. "The Renaissance seems to be everywhere. I know you're studying this important historical period in history, but Mrs. Bradley told me that her (2)___________________________ in her science classes is to discuss science and inventions of the Renaissance. "

Elsie added that in music class, Mrs. Denby planned to have the choir learn a Renaissance madrigal for the Spring Concert. "Furthermore," Ms. Steinman added, "I hear you all enjoyed Italian cuisine at lunch yesterday."

"From Mr. Clark, I know you are all (3)___________________________ of how the Renaissance period started as a movement in Italy in the 14th century after the more culturally (4)___________________________ period of the Middle Ages. Also, you are aware that there was a great revival of interest in ancient Rome and Greece during the Renaissance and that this interest extended into the art world. In architecture, for example, Brunelleschi studied the dimensions and sketches of Roman ruins and surviving buildings, as well as columns and arches. What began as a/an (5)___________________________ idea, eventually developed into architecture using classical ideas in new, innovative ways. Brunelleschi used his knowledge of the architecture of the classical past and created, among other buildings, the beautiful dome for the Cathedral of Santa Maria del Fiore in Florence, Italy, which can be seen today in all its beauty as a/an (6)___________________________ example of Renaissance architecture."

"Who can define perspective used in drawing?" asked Ms. Steinman.

Max correctly defined perspective as drawing in a way to give the effect of distance by showing objects on a two-dimensional surface in a way that gives the right impression of the height, width, depth, and position of those objects in relation to each other.

"Correct, Max. Brunelleschi also proposed a scientific theory of perspective. A friend of Brunelleschi, who traveled with him to Rome to study the style of the ancient Romans, was the sculptor, Donatello. Donatello mastered the art of sculpting in bronze. His bronze statue of David is the first large-scale, free-standing nude statue of the Renaissance, reminiscent of sculptures in ancient Greece and Rome. This Renaissance sculpture can be viewed in Florence, Italy, at the Museum of Bargello."

"What about painters?" inquired Hannah.

"Painters were also influenced by Renaissance ideas. Masaccio, for example, was a painter who showed a new freedom in the expression of emotion. His fresco, titled *Expulsion of Adam and Eve from Eden*, can be seen today in the Brancaccio Chapel inside the church of Santa Maria del Carmine in Florence. In this fresco, because of Masaccio's skill of portraying emotion, the shame of Adam and Eve almost seems (7)__________________________ and can be felt by the viewer. Also, another new element is the space around Adam and Eve. The background is part of a realistic landscape with a sense of depth because of the new interest in perspective."

"As you can imagine," Ms. Steinman reminded, "Thinking that we have finished discussing Renaissance art is (8)__________________________. Tomorrow, we'll talk about Leonardo da Vinci, Michelangelo, Raphael, and other important artists of this period. Even though da Vinci is my favorite artist, I promise to be (9)__________________________ and just present the facts about his life and his contributions not only to the world of art, but to science, engineering, anatomy, and I could go on and on. However, in the meantime, be (10)__________________________ and kind to each other."

### More Renaissance Sculptors

- Ghiberti – sculptor
- Nanni di Banco – sculptor in marble
- Michaelangelo – sculptor in marble
- Benvenuto Cellini – sculptor in bronze and gold
- Giambologna – sculptor in marble and bronze

**D.** The underlined part in each sentence is a synonym, idiom, phrase, or definition for a list word. Unscramble the list word and write the word on the blank.

1. In Ancient Greece, when Pythagoras first suggested that Earth was round, many people thought the idea was preposterous. ____________ dsuluoric
2. An important rule in journalism is to be unbiased when reporting the news. ____________ cejvibteo
3. Caroline's love of animals was obvious, because most of the photos she had on her iPhone were of her dog Rudy and her cat Cleopatra. ____________ lepalbap
4. According to Mr. Riley a creative writer is acutely observant of all of life. ____________ tgnoiazcn
5. Pentagon officials were extremely concerned that the foreign government was all-knowing about classified information when it was discovered that the Pentagon computer system had been hacked. ____________ ctosimenin
6. "Besides bears," explained Mrs. Bradley, "badgers, butterflies, bats, chipmunks, frogs, ladybugs, turtles, and wasps are some of the other animals that are dormant during the winter." ____________ nsequietc
7. Ms. Cosgrove's goal in physical education classes was to teach her students the skills necessary to understand or to participate in volleyball, tennis, basketball, golf, and soccer. ____________ oeecjvitb
8. After watching the movie *Time Out of Mind*, about the life of a homeless man living on the street and sleeping in a cardboard box, Ms. Palmer's students were compassionate about the plight of the homeless and organized a school-wide collection of blankets. ____________ uemnha
9. When they visited San Francisco, Harvey and Hope saw the Painted Ladies, a row of prototypical Victorian houses. ____________ icocin
10. The loquat seeds that Matthew planted for his botany project were still in an immature stage and had not sprouted. ____________ tinoecha

**E.** Write the word, idiom, or phrase from the choice box that best defines each list word.

- goal
- perceptive
- unnecessary
- evident
- inert
- absurd
- prototypical
- sympathetic
- nonpartisan
- embryonic
- all-knowing

1. iconic ____________________
2. quiescent ____________________
3. inchoate ____________________
4. cognizant ____________________
5. objective ____________________
6. palpable ____________________
7. humane ____________________
8. ludicrous ____________________
9. omniscient ____________________
10. objective ____________________

**F.** Complete each sentence to show that you understand the meaning of the underlined word.

1. Bella's objective in taking the summer class about coding and applications is to ________

_______________________________________________________________.

2. Ms. Cosgrove, the gym teacher, wanted all of her students to be cognizant of __________

_______________________________________________________________.

3. An iconic destination for world travelers is ______________________________________

_______________________________________________________________.

4. It is important to be objective when ______________________________________

_______________________________________________________________.

5. In her persuasive essay, Milly argued for the humane ______________________________

_______________________________________________________________.

6. Students thought that Principal Zhang was omniscient because ______________________

_______________________________________________________________.

7. Casey never seems to be quiescent; instead he ______________________________

_______________________________________________________________.

8. "What a ludicrous idea," laughed Mandy when Matt told her ______________________

_______________________________________________________________.

9. We could tell that the painting that Max was working on was in an inchoate stage because

_______________________________________________________________.

10. When Ms. Palmer's drama class learned that they were taking a trip to Broadway in New York City, to see three plays during spring break, their feelings were palpable by the way they _______________________________________________________.

# Review: Lists 9-12

**A.** Use the clues to complete the crossword puzzle with vocabulary words, synonyms, or information from the activities.

**Across**

1. Ancestry
6. Embody
7. Idiosyncrasy
9. Humane
13. Treason
14. Undeveloped

**Down**

1. Shock into action
2. Ludicrous
3. Erase
4. Gesticulate
5. Relating to a symbol
8. Deflect
10. Being unknown
11. Alienate
12. Fabrication

**B.** Circle the answer which best completes the sentence.

1. She was **culpable** of
   a. riding the bus.
   b. stealing the bracelet
   c. preparing breakfast.

2. He was **condescending** in the way he
   a. tied his shoes.
   b. did the Irish jig.
   c. talked to his female employees.

3. As a **gratuity**, the hotel
   a. offered a free breakfast buffet.
   b. overcharged its guests.
   c. was situated near the ocean.

4. In a **retrospective** mood, she
   a. showed all her friends her new shoes.
   b. talked about her childhood.
   c. applauded for the singer.

5. An **incisive** remark might be a
   a. compliment.
   b. luncheon invitation.
   c. criticism.

6. An **unctuous** person is probably not
   a. sincere.
   b. ingratiating.
   c. slippery.

7. A **unanimous** vote means
   a. all in agreement.
   b. all in disagreement.
   c. an invalid vote.

8. One might **confer** with a
   a. counselor.
   b. pair of shoes.
   c. plate of broccoli.

9. **Gastronomy** is the study of
   a. the Bible.
   b. stomach ailments.
   c. foods.

10. A scene with **pathos** would evoke
    a. humor.
    b. absurdity.
    c. sadness.

11. Something **palpable** is a
    a. dream.
    b. wart on someone's nose.
    c. memory.

12. A **quiescent** person might be
    a. dancing.
    b. cheering at a volleyball game.
    c. taking a nap on the sofa.

13. In literature **omniscient** could describe
    a. the plot.
    b. the exposition.
    c. the point of view.

14. **Objective** reporting includes
    a. facts.
    b. opinion.
    c. gossip.

**C.** Write the best word that might be included in the news story for each headline.

| | | |
|---|---|---|
| quandary | confer | quiescent |
| manifesto | obsolescence | objective |
| aplomb | prehensile | corroborate |
| gratuitous | arbitrary | cognizant |

1. ______________________ "Local Police Make Seniors Aware of Scams in Area"

2. ______________________ "Washington Zoo Acquires a Pair of Central American Kinkajous"

3. ______________________ "Unnecessary Violence Mars a Promising Movie"

4. ______________________ "Washington Post Staff Wins 2016 Pulitzer Prize in Journalism"

5. ______________________ "Suspect Free of Charges When Key Witness Supports Her Alibi"

6. ______________________ "The President Outlines his Plans for the Nation in Labor Day Speech"

7. ______________________ "Display of Inventions From the Past at the National Museum of American History"

8. ______________________ "Inactive Volcano Erupts Unexpectedly"

9. ______________________ "City Council Perplexed about Sinkholes Appearing on City Streets"

10. ______________________ "Local Tennis Player's Goal is to Bring Home Wimbledon Trophy"

11. ______________________ "Officials Consider Choices for Sites of 2020 Winter Olympics"

# Vocabulary List 13
## Noble Nouns

| **Word**<br>[pronunciation]<br>**other word form**<br> | **Definition**<br>• sample sentence<br> |
|---|---|
| **aplomb**<br>[uh PLUHM] | poise, confidence, and self-assurance<br>• With aplomb, she addressed the student body. |
| **coercion**<br>[ko UR shuhn]<br>**coerce** (v) | use of force or intimidation to obtain compliance<br>• The government used coercion to discourage criticism. |
| **discord**<br>[DIS kawrd]<br>**discordant** (adj) | [1]disagreement between people [2]lack of harmony in music<br>• [1]Family discord surfaced whenever they discussed politics.<br>• [2]Tuning musical instruments results in a sound of discord. |
| **fait accompli**<br>[feyt ah KOM plee] | an irreversible fact, action, or decision<br>• The family into which one is born is fait accompli, but each individual has his or her own personality. |
| **interlocutor**<br>[in ter LOK yuh ter] | one who takes part in a conversation<br>• A good interlocutor is skilled at both speaking and listening. |
| **jurisprudence**<br>[joor is PROOD ens] | a body or system of laws<br>• The Supreme Court is the ultimate jurisprudence in the U.S. |
| **parasite**<br>[PAR uh sahyt]<br>**parasitic** (adj) | [1]an organism that lives in or on another organism known as the host<br>[2]a person who relies on or exploits another<br>• [1]Malaria is a disease that is caused by a parasite.<br>• [2]"You are a parasite," accused Becky when Casey asked her again if he could copy her math homework. |
| **peccadillo**<br>[pek uh DIL oh] | a small mistake, fault, or offense<br>• "Neglecting to close the refrigerator door is not a peccadillo," Mom angrily told Bernie. |
| **tome**<br>[tohm] | a large, heavy, scholarly book<br>• The tome titled, *Impressionism Illustrated*, could have been used as a doorstop. |

**A.** Decide if the underlined words are used correctly or incorrectly in the sentences below. Write Correct or Incorrect on the blank.

1. ______________________ The mother used <u>coercion</u> by promising her toddler a cookie if he would behave.

2. ______________________ Taking a bribe to change a vote would be a <u>peccadillo</u> for a U.S. senator.

3. ______________________ He studied <u>jurisprudence</u> in the College of Pharmacy.

4. ______________________ A <u>parasite</u> would be best described as dependent.

5. ______________________ When there was <u>discord</u> in the family, everyone was happy.

6. ______________________ The six-volume *The Decline and Fall of the Roman Empire* might be considered a <u>tome</u>.

7. ______________________ Mrs. Bradley selected the <u>interlocutor</u>, Mandy, to lead the discussion.

8. ______________________ "Your essay grade is a <u>fait accompli</u>," said Ms. Patterson. "You have the chance to revise it for a better grade."

9. ______________________ His <u>aplomb</u> was obvious by his quavering voice and shaking hands when he gave his speech.

10. ______________________ The sound of the orchestra tuning their instruments was one of <u>discord</u>.

11. ______________________ A person who is a <u>parasite</u> would never ask another for something.

**B.** Write the best word from the choice box to complete each sentence.

| | | | |
|---|---|---|---|
| aplomb | fait accompli | tome | peccadillo |
| coerce | interlocutor | parasitic | pandemic |
| discordant | jurisprudence | | |

1. Milly's sister, who was considering a career in law, was taking a course titled "An Introduction to ____________________________" at UCLA.

2. "It's not fair to say I'm ________________________ just because I borrowed some paper today and asked if you had an extra pencil," complained Max.

3. Mr. Greenberg, who coached the tennis team, said their recent defeat was a/an ___________________________ but with more practice and tactical drills to improve accuracy, the team could win future matches.

4. With _________________________, Milly walked onto the stage, bowed to the audience, took her seat at the piano, and began to play Rachmaninoff's "Piano Concerto No. 2."

5. Mandy, who tried to impress her classmates with her extensive vocabulary, sat down with her discussion group and declared, "As a/an _______________________, I am predisposed to augment my dialogue with my wealth of erudition."

6. Aiden, a history fan, said that the book *Hamilton* by Ron Chernow was a _________________________ well worth reading.

7. In *A Christmas Carol* by Charles Dickens, Ebenezer Scrooge is visited in a dream by three spirits of Christmas who ___________________________ him into seeing his past, present, and future, hoping to change his nasty, miserly treatment of other people.

8. "Kara," pleaded Matt, "the fact that I forgot to call you last night was only a/an ____________________________, not a serious offense."

9. "Let's avoid the topic of politics during Thanksgiving dinner, because political discussions seem to lead to a/an ________________________ argument," warned Emmalin's dad.

 

## C. Story Challenge

Write the best word from the choice box to fill each blank in the story.

| | | | |
|---|---|---|---|
| aplomb | idiosyncrasy | parasite | tomes |
| fait accompli | interlocutor | parasite | discord |
| discord | jurisprudence | peccadillo | coercion |

### Awareness of Allusions

The focus of today's lesson in Mr. Stewart's literature class was allusions. Before beginning the lesson, Mr. Stewart first closed the door to avoid being disturbed by the (1)______________________________ of students tuning their instruments in the music room down the hall. Then he asked the class if anyone knew the definition of a literary allusion. Max raised his hand.

"When we read *To Kill a Mockingbird*, Max recalled, Scout got in trouble with her teacher when she identifies a 'cootie' crawling out of Burris Ewell's hair. Cootie was a term used for head lice, a real organism that was a/an (2)______________________________. My grandma said that the word later became used in the popular culture of her time as an imaginary disease carried by someone of the opposite sex. She still remembers whispering to her grade school friends, 'He's got cooties,' and running in the opposite direction. I think the word cooties would be an allusion."

"You're correct, Max. Allusions come from a variety of sources. What I would like you to do is to copy the week's vocabulary words and definitions into your notebooks, and then we'll use the words in today's lesson about allusions."

"Which character in the *Harry Potter* series was named after the daughter of Helen of Troy from Greek mythology?" Mr. Stewart asked.

Rachel, a *Harry Potter* fan, knew the answer. "Hermione," she said. "In Greek mythology, Hermione was an intelligent girl who was good at strategy and planning, so the name fits," Rachel explained.

"Exactly, Rachel. <u>The naming of a character or any other brief and indirect reference to a person, place, thing, or idea from another source is called allusion</u>," Mr. Stewart explained. "A source can be mythological as in the case of Hermione or cultural such as Max's example of cootie. Additionally, in our reading, we may come across allusions to history, literature, politics, art, and music."

Mr. Stewart challenged his class to think of allusions using the vocabulary words and to compose a sentence with the word that would be common in everyday life.

"Like a suitor of Penelope, the young man continued to live off of his parents like a/an (3)______________________________ instead of getting a job," said Dylan.

"Can anyone explain Dylan's allusion?" asked Mr. Stewart.

"We read *The Odyssey*, and while Odysseus was away fighting in the Greek-Trojan War, some men of Ithaca took advantage of his absence and moved into his palace, eating his food and courting his wife Penelope," Caroline interpreted. "The suitors used (4)______________________________, threatening to stay in the palace until Penelope admitted Odysseus was dead and took one of them as her husband."

Hannah asked to be next. "Like Napoleon Bonaparte, the student was a bookworm reading (5)______________________________ from all periods in history." Hannah explained that in history class, Mr. Clark said that Napoleon had a personal librarian and carried a portable library with him always.

Gary had an example. "Joanna caused (6)______________________________. Like Eris, she liked to stir up jealousy among her friends." Everyone understood Gary's example, because they knew the Greek story about how Eris threw a golden apple into the center of a wedding banquet on which the words "For the Fairest" were printed. This apple caused jealousy between three beautiful goddesses—Hera, Aphrodite, and Athena—each thought the apple was intended for her.

Suzanne was next, "Like a Trojan horse, the election of the new president was a/an (7)______________________________. His election was final and some people thought that undesirable consequences were sure to come."

"During the war between Greece and Troy, the Greeks rolled a gargantuan wooden Trojan horse into the walls of Troy, pretending that this horse was a gift," Suzanne explained. "However, once the Trojans accepted the gift horse, it was too late to reject the offer, and they were devastated when they realized that an army of Greek soldiers was hidden within the horse," she concluded.

"I have an example," said Ned. "Being grilled by my dad about where I was going, who I was going with, and when I would be home is like a lesson in Draconian (8)______________________________." Ned explained that a grilling by his dad was like being before judges in ancient Greece who used the brutal code of law of Draco."

Heidi was anxious to give her example. "Even though he speaks and acts with

(9)___________________________, he is not narcissistic." Heidi explained that her allusion was from mythology, and that Narcissus was an arrogant, conceited young man.

Milly wanted to be next. "Like Pandora, Joseph's curiosity seemed like a harmless (10)___________________________. He wanted to see what his cockatoo would do if he opened the cage, and that led to disaster when it flew away out of the open window."

Casey was eager to explain Milly's allusion. "Pandora's curiosity made her open a box when she was ordered not to. By doing this she released evil into the world."

Ann wanted to do a word. "Even though he was a gifted (11)______________________, it was a wonder his nose didn't grow longer as he talked, because his conversation was often filled with exaggerations and half-truths."

Ann explained that even though the name Pinocchio wasn't mentioned, the reference to the nose growing longer was a recognizable allusion from a children's novel.

"Excellent work, class," said Mr. Stewart. "Keep your eyes and ears open for allusions when you read and listen and have a great day," he said as class ended.

Some Origins of Allusions

- literature
- history
- popular culture
- mythology
- the Bible
- speeches

**D.** The underlined part in each sentence is a synonym, idiom, phrase, or definition for a list word. Unscramble the list word and write the word on the blank.

1. When Bridget was interviewed for a summer apprenticeship at a local veterinary clinic, the doctor was impressed with her <u>poise</u> and experience working with animals. ____________________ mlabpo

2. Whenever <u>disagreements</u> occurred between her friends, Mandy was the peacemaker who encouraged them to openly discuss hard feelings. ____________________ ridodsc

3. Mom used <u>forceful persuasion</u> by reminding Eli that time spent playing video games would be seriously jeopardized if he didn't improve his English grade. ____________________ ecnocori

4. Ms. Liu reminded her history class that after the <u>end result</u>, which was a Union victory in the Civil War, it was time to heal the divided country. ____________________ ctapiaicfolm

5. "Turning in one math assignment late is a <u>small mistake</u>," reminded Mrs. Ocho. "Frequently turning in assignments late, however, will seriously impact your grade." ____________________ copcleadli

6. "This is a <u>large book</u>," complained Josh when Mr. Nelson assigned Tolstoy's *War and Peace* as the novel to be read during spring break. ____________________ emto

7. Some think that when a whale breaches the water and does a flop, it is trying to rid itself of barnacles, a shelled marine <u>animal that often lives off of another larger animal</u>. ____________________ saetrapi

8. Dylan's brother Danny was studying medical <u>legislation</u>, the science of law as applied to the practice of medicine. ____________________ duisjrceunrpe

9. "I would like you all to become <u>conversationalists</u> and discuss with your groups resolutions that we could use in debating," instructed Ms. Palmer. ____________________ trsieountrloc

10. The <u>lack of harmony</u> from tuning instruments ended when the maestro lifted his baton. ____________________ rodsidc

11. Matt was tired of Gary being a <u>borrower</u> by continually asking to borrow either a pencil, paper, or lunch money each day. ____________________ repaasti

**E.** Write the word, idiom, or phrase from the choice box that best defines each list word.

- science of law
- conversationalist
- ancestry
- lack of harmony
- forceful persuasion
- disagreement
- dependent organism
- irrevocable
- exploits others
- heavy book
- poise
- small mistake

1. aplomb ____________________
2. interlocutor ____________________
3. coercion ____________________
4. parasite ____________________
5. tome ____________________
6. peccadillo ____________________
7. fait accompli ____________________
8. discord ____________________
9. jurisprudence ____________________
10. discord ____________________
11. parasite ____________________

**F.** Complete each sentence to show that you understand the meaning of the underlined word.

1. A cause of discord between friends might be ______________________________
______________________________________________________________.

2. A book that would resemble a tome is ______________________________
______________________________________________________________.

3. One could tell that Brendan was a young man with aplomb because he ________________
______________________________________________________________.

4. Mr. Clark said that in history, a time when coercion was necessary was ________________
______________________________________________________________.

5. Mandy said that her friend's only peccadillo was ______________________________
______________________________________________________________.

6. "Fait accompli," said a group of students when they ______________________________
______________________________________________________________.

7. The students agreed that a summer job that would be valuable for a career in jurisprudence is ______________________________
______________________________________________________________.

8. Ms. Palmer said that two skills needed by an interlocutor are ______________________________
______________________________________________________________.

9. Dylan said his older brother Danny was a parasite because ______________________________
______________________________________________________________.

10. Musical discord is sometimes heard in Milly's home when ______________________________
______________________________________________________________.

11. An example of an organism that is a parasite is ______________________________
______________________________________________________________.

# Vocabulary List 14
## Awesome Adjectives

| **Word**<br>[pronunciation]<br>**other word form**<br> | **Definition**<br>• sample sentence<br> |
|---|---|
| **ambivalent**<br>[am BIV uh luhnt]<br>**ambivalence** (n) | having simultaneous and contradictory feelings toward someone or something<br>• Heidi was ambivalent about Tim; sometimes she liked him, but often, she thought he was rude. |
| **caustic**<br>[KAW stik] | [1]capable of burning, corroding, or destroying living tissue<br>[2]sarcastic in a scathing or bitter way<br>• [1]The directions on the box of caustic cleaner said to use caution when using.<br>• [2]The editorial criticizing the senator was caustic in tone. |
| **cursory**<br>[KUR suh ree] | going rapidly over something without attention to details<br>• John's cursory look at the assigned short story was not enough to pass the quiz. |
| **contemptible**<br>[kuhn TEMP tuh buhl]<br>**contempt** (n) | very bad and deserving of scorn<br>• Many people thought the actions of the protestors were contemptible. |
| **dogmatic**<br>[dawg MAT ik]<br>**dogma** (n) | expressing personal beliefs or opinions as if they cannot be disputed<br>• Celeste's father was dogmatic about how he expected his children to behave. |
| **empathetic**<br>[em puh THET ik]<br>**empathy** (n) | the ability to understand and share the feelings of another<br>• Christina was empathetic to new students, because she was once a new student when she moved from New Jersey. |
| **euphonious**<br>[you FOH nee uhs]<br>**euphony** (n) | a sound that is pleasing to the ear<br>• A euphonious sound came from the music room as the Glee Club sang "The Battle Hymn of the Republic." |
| **succinct**<br>[suhk SINGKT] | using few words to express an idea<br>• Author Ernest Hemingway is known for his succinct style of writing. |
| **verdant**<br>[VUR dunt] | green with growing plants<br>• Rachel's parents rode in a cable car over a verdant rainforest in Costa Rica. |

**A.** Write the best list word that the synonyms, idioms, or phrases define to complete each sentence.

| ambivalent | cursory | dogmatic | caustic |
|---|---|---|---|
| verdant | empathetic | euphonious | iconic |
| caustic | contemptible | succinct | |

1. Luke asked his dad if he could use the family car to drive a group of friends to a concert, and his dad replied with a/an ____________________________, "No."

   brief terse to the point concise

2. Ms. Denby finds the sounds of nature ____________________________ and plays an album of music titled "Calming Rain With Distant Thunder," to fall asleep at night.

   melodious harmonious dulcet mellifluous

3. Bella was ____________________________ about the lunch choices of tofu salad and parsnip stew.

   hesitant indecisive ambiguous uncertain

4. "Anyone who makes fun of a disabled person is a/an ____________________________ person," affirmed Celeste.

   despicable outrageous heinous vile

5. When Casey's dog died, Elsie was ____________________________ and offered support, because she remembered how she felt when her dog died.

   sympathetic compassionate understanding sensitive

6. The ____________________________ comedy sketch made fun of hypocrisy and partisanship in politics.

   acrimonious acerbic sharp biting

7. Central Park is a/an ____________________________ oasis in the busy, urban city of New York.

   blooming lush flourishing grassy

8. Mrs. Bradley says it is absurd to be ____________________________ about science, because with new discoveries, ideas can change.

   opinionated intolerant authoritarian pigheaded

9. Mr. Riley quickly took a/an ____________________________ look through the research papers to make sure his students had included a works cited page.

   hasty careless slapdash perfunctory

10. Sodium hydroxide is a/an ____________________________ substance found in household products such as oven cleaners, drain cleaners, and some detergents.

    abrasive acerbic irritating stinging

**B.** Write the best word from the choice box to complete each sentence.

| | | | |
|---|---|---|---|
| verdant | autodidactic | caustic | dogma |
| cursory | ambivalence | succinct | contempt |
| caustic | empathy | euphony | |

1. Ms. Paterson reminded her students that plagiarism was an error in judgment that was worthy of __________________________ and would result in negative consequences.

2. Milly, a gifted pianist, also sang with __________________________.

3. On vacation, Heidi experienced __________________________; she wanted to see the view from the top of the Eiffel Tower in Paris, but she was frightened of heights.

4. "Mandy is such a know-it-all," Rachel complained to Celeste. "She thinks everything she says is __________________________ and no one dares to disagree with her."

5. Cindy had a rash on her hands after scrubbing the bathroom with a/an __________________________ cleaner.

6. When Hillary got braces, Gary had __________________________ for her because he remembered that when he had them, they were uncomfortable at first and difficult to get used to.

7. "When you proofread your essays, a/an __________________________ look is not enough," reminded Ms. Paterson.

8. "Being __________________________ is getting to the point without wasting words," prompted Ms. Paterson after explaining the essay assignment.

9. When Luke asked Suzanne if he could copy her math homework, her __________________________ reply, "Do your own work," took him by surprise.

10. "Everything looked dry and withered before, but after a week of rain the landscape looks __________________________," observed Ms. Cosgrove.

## C. Story Challenge

Write the best word from the choice box to fill each blank in the story.

| | | | |
|---|---|---|---|
| caustic | facetious | empathetic | verdant |
| ambivalent | dogmatic | euphonious | caustic |
| cursory | contemptible | succinct | |

### From Allusion to Irony

As the students entered Mr. Stewart's world literature class, Max was complaining, but trying to impress Mr. Stewart by using an allusion in his complaint. "I feel like Sisyphus," he said. "Just when I think I've caught up with all my schoolwork, some teacher gives another big assignment." Shane was (1)______________________________ to him. "I know what you mean," he said, "I feel the same."

"So who was Sisyphus, Max?" asked Mr. Stewart.

"Some Greek king who was probably guilty of hubris and was punished by the gods by being forced to roll a huge rock up a hill, only to have it roll back down the hill. And to make matters worse, the gods made him repeat this for all eternity," said Max.

"I'm impressed, Max—hubris and allusion?" After the class was all seated and attendance had been taken, Mr. Stewart began. "Today, we'll discuss irony, a figure of speech in which words are spoken or actions occur that are the opposite of what the words or actions really mean. There are three important kinds of irony," Mr. Stewart continued. "Verbal irony is a figure of speech in which a person says one thing but means the opposite, situational irony is when something happens that is the opposite of what is expected, and dramatic irony is when the audience or reader knows something that the characters do not know."

"Look at the week's vocabulary words. Do you know which word connects in some way to irony?" asked Mr. Stewart.

"(2)______________________________," said Michael, "because irony is a contradiction in speech or situation, and the word means a contradiction."

"Very perceptive, Michael," said Mr. Stewart. "To help you understand, I'll begin with an example and then ask all of you to provide some examples."

"When we read Edgar Allen Poe's short story, 'The Cask of Amontillado,' you may remember the main character's name was Fortunato," said Mr. Stewart. "Can anyone recall why his name would be an example of verbal irony?"

 

Becky volunteered to answer. "Fortunato was anything but fortunate—in fact just the opposite. He ended up deliberately trapped in a dank, dark wine cellar by a guy who wanted revenge."

"I have an example of verbal irony," said Aiden. "We studied the Roaring Twenties in America in history class, and one of the most vicious gangsters during that time who committed (3)______________________________ crimes was called Baby Face Nelson. You don't expect a guy called Baby Face to be a really bad criminal."

When Hillary said her examples were from the movie *Finding Nemo*, everyone laughed, but Mr. Stewart said that many examples of irony can be found in *Finding Nemo*. "In fact," he said, "we are all going to watch the Disney movie, *Zootopia* to find examples of irony and other literary devices."

Hillary said the clownfish in *Finding Nemo* was very unfriendly, and the pelican was a friend with the fish. "You wouldn't expect a fish with a name such as clownfish to be unfriendly, so the name would be verbal irony and traditionally, pelicans dine on fish, so a pelican-fish friendship would be situational irony."

"Good examples Hillary. Brendan, you look eager. Do you have an example or did this mention of dining make you hungry and anxious for lunch period?"

"My example is situational irony," said Brendan. "When we read *The Odyssey,* I remember the story of the Sirens who, from a distance looked like beautiful women singing with (4)______________________________ voices, but instead they were horrible, evil hags who wanted to devour Odysseus and his crew."

Mandy also had an example of situational irony. "We read *A Christmas Carol* last year," she said. "Ebenezer Scrooge seemed like an old curmudgeon who talked to everyone in a/an (5)______________________________ way, so seeing him turn into a man with love and joy in his heart who treats others with kindness is unexpected. I think this is situational irony," said Mandy.

"I think you're correct, Mandy," said Mr. Stewart.

"I think political candidates often use verbal irony," observed Christopher. "They seem to make these (6)______________________________ statements about what they will do if they're elected, and then sometimes they do the opposite once they are in office."

"A good practical example and unfortunately sometimes true," said Mr. Stewart.

"We read a story titled 'The Most Dangerous Game' last year," said Harvey. "The setting was a beautiful (7)______________________________ lush island, but behind the scenes of this paradise-like setting, hunting and killing humans took place as a 'game' to the Russian aristocrat, Zaroff. I think that's situational irony," said Harvey, "because the reader doesn't expect horrible things to happen on such a beautiful island."

"Good examples, class. Another example is from a poem we read by Samuel Taylor Coleridge called "The Rime of the Ancient Mariner." A line in the poem is 'Water, water, everywhere/Nor any drop to drink.' This idea is definitely situational irony—the idea that the thirsty sailors are surrounded by water but can't drink the ocean's salt water," explained Mr. Stewart.

"Also," explained Mr. Stewart, "an example of dramatic irony is in Shakespeare's *MacBeth*. King Duncan says he trusts MacBeth. However, Duncan doesn't know that the three witches prophesied that MacBeth would become king and that he would rise to the throne by killing Duncan. The audience knows about the witches and Duncan's fate even though Duncan is not aware of what's in store for him."

"For our next class period I would like you to read the short story, 'The Necklace,' by Guy de Maupassant and to write a/an (8)____________________________ one page essay analyzing the irony in the story. Just a reminder, (9)____________________________ reading will not do; you must read the story carefully to understand the irony," Mr. Stewart said as class ended.

As the students were about to leave, the PA came on with an announcement from Principal Zhang. "Remember, all physical education classes will be held outside today and tomorrow, as the smell from the (10)____________________________ sealer used for the gym floor dissipates. And, do something nice for someone today," he reminded.

Types of Irony

- verbal irony
- situational irony
- dramatic irony

**D.** The underlined part in each sentence is a synonym, idiom, phrase, or definition for a list word. Unscramble the list word and write the word on the blank.

1. The new fountain that was installed in the school courtyard produced a pleasantly soothing sound. ________________ unohiesupo

2. In art class, Max painted a seascape using shades of indigo blue and grass green. ________________ nrtavde

3. Aiden was very opinionated when he said, "Without a doubt, history is the most important subject in school." ________________ moctdiga

4. Mr. Clark was compassionate toward refugees fleeing from war-torn countries. ________________ heptecimat

5. Ms. Paterson gave each student in his composition class a handout that explained the rules of grammar and punctuation in a concise way. ________________ nuctcsic

6. The food critic wrote an acrimonious review of the new restaurant criticizing the food and service. ________________ tcasuci

7. "The number of outrageous errors in spelling and grammar in your essays is inexcusable," criticized Ms. Paterson. ________________ poitlcntebem

8. Because she only took a hasty look at the recipe, Julia used baking soda instead of baking powder and ruined the cake she was baking. ________________ ourycsr

9. Casey's father was uncertain about accepting the promotion at work; he knew he would make more money, but the added responsibility would mean less time with his family. ________________ tembilavna

10. Suzanne always made sure that abrasive household products could not be reached by the children for whom she babysat. ________________ ucsctai

**E.** Write the word, idiom, or phrase from the choice box that best defines each list word.

- acerbic
- contradictory
- able to grasp
- superficially
- opinionated
- very bad
- compassionate
- harmonious
- sarcastic
- green
- pithy

1. empathetic ______________________
2. cursory ______________________
3. succinct ______________________
4. contemptible ______________________
5. caustic ______________________
6. dogmatic ______________________
7. verdant ______________________
8. ambivalent ______________________
9. euphonious ______________________
10. caustic ______________________

 

**F.** Complete each sentence to show that you understand the meaning of the underlined word.

1. The park could be described as verdant because ________________________________

________________________________________________________________.

2. Ms. Paterson explained that writing in a succinct way means ________________________

________________________________________________________________.

3. Dylan had ambivalent feelings about ________________________________________

________________________________________________________________.

4. Euphonious sounds came from the auditorium when ______________________________

________________________________________________________________.

5. Mr. Clark reminded students that a cursory look would not be enough when ____________

________________________________________________________________.

6. Emmalin said she experiences empathetic feelings whenever she ____________________

________________________________________________________________.

7. A dogmatic rule of Brendan's parents is ____________________________________

________________________________________________________________.

8. "A behavior that I consider contemptible is ____________________________________

__________________________________________________________," explained John.

9. Ms. Cosgrove's caustic response when Luke tripped Tim in gym class was, " ____________

________________________________________________________________."

10. Casey said that a caustic product kept in their garage is ____________________________

________________________________________________________________.

# Vocabulary List 15
## Volatile Verbs

| **Word**<br>[pronunciation]<br>**other word form** | **Definition**<br>• sample sentence |
|---|---|
|  |  |
| **advocate**<br>[AD vuh keyt] | to speak or write in favor of<br>• Ms. Cosgrove advocated serving healthy foods in the cafeteria. |
| **conform**<br>[kuhn FAWRM]<br>**conformity** (n) | to be obedient or compliant<br>• Students were expected to conform to rules for decorating lockers. |
| **emulate**<br>[EM yuh leyt] | to try to equal or excel<br>• Dylan hoped to emulate his brother Danny's academic success. |
| **extrapolate**<br>[ik STRAP uh leyt] | to make a guess about what might happen based on prior information<br>• Ms. Palmer extrapolated that the school quiz bowl team would triumph. |
| **jeopardize**<br>[JEP er diyz] | to expose to danger or risk<br>• Max knew if he didn't get an A on the history test, he would jeopardize his grade average. |
| **reciprocate**<br>[ree SIP ruh keyt] | to mutually give and take<br>• Bella received a gift from her aunt and reciprocated with a thank you card. |
| **reconcile**<br>[REK uhn siyl]<br>**reconciliation** (n) | [1]to settle a disagreement [2]to accept or submit to something considered unpleasant<br>• [1]After an argument, Rachel and Cindy reconciled.<br>• [2]Gary was reconciled to the fact that he could not finish his research paper on time. |
| **undermine**<br>[uhn der MIYN] | to weaken, injure, or impair, often by stealthy or insidious means<br>• False rumors undermined the reputation of the senator. |
| **waive**<br>[weyv] | to choose to, or allow someone to, disregard a rule, right, or claim<br>• Symphony ticket fees were waived for Mrs. Denby's music students. |

**A.** Write synonyms or antonyms before each pair of words.

1. ______________________________ jeopardize – protect
2. ______________________________ reconcile – accept
3. ______________________________ extrapolate – hypothesize
4. ______________________________ conform – adapt
5. ______________________________ undermine – assist
6. ______________________________ reciprocate – exchange
7. ______________________________ emulate – mimic
8. ______________________________ advocate – oppose
9. ______________________________ reconcile – disagree
10. ______________________________ waive – disregard

**B.** Write the best word from the choice box to complete each sentence.

| | | | |
|---|---|---|---|
| undermine | waived | advocated | reciprocated |
| reconciliation | emulated | extrapolating | jeopardize |
| litigate | conformity | | |

1. The defendant ____________________________ his right to have a lawyer, and declared he would be responsible for his own legal representation.

2. On career day, a social worker who ____________________________ for foster children, spoke to a group of students.

3. Coach Greenberg warned the basketball team that failure to play harmoniously as a team would ______________________________ their success.

4. Ned had a ____________________________ with Mr. Clark after he apologized for making a disrespectful remark in class.

5. In speech class, Ms. Palmer warned that posting inappropriate pictures on Facebook could ______________________________ safety and reputation.

6. Both Justin and Elsie enjoyed ___________________________ which college basketball teams would be successful in the NCAA March Madness tournament.

7. ___________________________ was not important to Milly when it came to the current teenage fashion trends and instead she dressed in her own unique way.

8. At lunch, Rachel shared her walnut brownies with Elsie, and she ____________________________ by giving Rachel half of her ham and cheese sandwich.

9. Bella's little sister Shannon ___________________________ everything she did.

 

## C. Story Challenge

Write the best word from the choice box to fill each blank in the story.

| | | | |
|---|---|---|---|
| extrapolated | confer | conform | advocated |
| waiving | emulate | jeopardized | reconcile |
| reconciled | undermine | reciprocated | |

### Renaissance Artists

Ms. Steinman began the discussion about Renaissance artists by reminding her students that humanists (1)________________________ human achievements as well as the ingenuity and effort that went into their efforts. She explained that because of this appreciation of human accomplishments, more time was spent on work that would benefit people in their daily lives.

"Today," Ms. Steinman continued, "We will focus on some artists and show how their lives and art (2)________________________ the new way of thinking during the Renaissance period."

"For example," she began, "Leonardo Da Vinci is often referred to as a Renaissance man because he was not (3)________________________ to simply being an artist. He had exceptional talent in a wide range of fields. Not only was he talented in the visual arts, but he was a scientist as well. Da Vinci's famous sketchbooks show original designs for bridges, weapons, engines, and vehicles. From these sketches, we know that he even (4)________________________ that in the future there would be flying machines."

"In his famous painting, the *Last Supper*, Da Vinci did not (5)____________________ by continuing painting styles of the past, but instead followed the ideas of Masaccio and others and showed drama and feeling in his work. For example, emotions are obvious in the faces of Jesus and his apostles at the Last Supper."

"(6) ________________________ the previously accepted way of painting," Ms. Steinman continued, "Da Vinci also introduced a new effect in which he gently blurred his colors to avoid hard lines and to more accurately portray light and shadow. This effect is known as 'sfumato,' which means smoky. In another of Da Vinci's famous paintings—the *Mona Lisa*—we see this effect in the dream-like rocky background."

"Artists did not attempt to (7)____________________________ the innovations of their predecessors," Ms. Steinman explained, "but instead adapted new ideas based on their predecessor's art work. For example, the background in Da Vinci's *Mona Lisa* uses Masaccio's technique of creating a believable open space for the background, but uses the new technique of 'sfumato.'"

"Another Renaissance artist known for his sculptures and his painting was Michelangelo," Ms. Steinman added. "His father thought that a career in the arts was below the family's social status, so he encouraged his son to pursue a career in business. Michelangelo, however, defied his father by becoming an artist and was never able to (8)____________________________ with his father during his life. He studied sculpture and anatomy and later carved *The Pieta*, a sculpture of Mary supporting the crucified Christ across her knees. By 1501, Michelangelo became recognized as the most talented sculptor of central Italy and was commissioned to carve a statue of the Biblical hero *David*, for the Florence Cathedral."

"Possibly his most famous art work, however, was not a sculpture but a painting—the 12,000 foot ceiling of the Sistine Chapel in the Vatican in Rome, Italy. This painting took him more than four years to complete and depicted various scenes from the biblical Book of Genesis such as *The Creation of Adam*. Michelangelo's health was seriously (9)____________________________ during this time from working in extremely uncomfortable conditions in physical discomfort with his head continually tilted upward."

"The hardships on behalf of his art were worthwhile because people (10)____________________________ by regarding Michelangelo as one of the greatest masters of the Renaissance period."

As class ended, Ms. Steinman promised to continue the discussion of Renaissance art.

### Renaissance Art Jargon

- fresco – painting directly into wet plaster
- contrapposto – painting or sculpting a figure in a natural pose
- chiaroscuro – use of light and shade in painting
- impasto – thickly applied paint
- tondo – a circular painting or sculpture

**D.** The underlined part in each sentence is a synonym, idiom, phrase, or definition for a list word. Unscramble the list word and write the word on the blank.

1. Heidi learned that the king was the most important piece in chess and if it is endangered, moves must be made to make it safe immediately. ______ ordezeaidjp

2. Mrs. Bradley estimated that half of her class would pass the science test; consequently, she was happily surprised when each student earned a passing grade. ______ dxetptalaoer

3. Mr. Collins, a school counselor, recommended a summer class in human anatomy to Max to practice drawing the human body. ______ taecdadvo

4. Principal Zhang overlooked the uniform dress code on "Book Blitz Day," when students dressed like a favorite character from a book. ______ aviedw

5. In the mid-1800s, American author Henry David Thoreau refused to comply to ideas supporting slavery and American imperialism. ______ orncmfo

6. During WWII, after Japan's attack on Pearl Harbor, President Franklin D. Roosevelt ordered many Japanese-Americans to be relocated and imprisoned because of the fear they might sabotage the country. ______ eenurindm

7. When Hannah was sick, Hope offered to work her shift as a lifeguard at the YMCA pool, and Hannah returned the favor by taking Hope's shift when she wanted to spend time with her brother, who had been away at college. ______ croapeecrtid

8. Coach Greenberg invited Cindy and Milly into his office to try to make peace between the two friends who had a noisy argument after a tennis match. ______ rclecioen

9. "I have to be careful of each thing I say and do," sighed Becky. "My little sister Marissa continually imitates me." ______ utsealem

10. Piper wanted a dog, but her brother Charlie was allergic to animals with fur, so Piper was resigned to having two parakeets – Mango and Kiwi. ______ ldrcineoec

**E.** Write the word, idiom, or phrase from the choice box that best defines each list word.

- recommend
- model oneself on
- estimate
- put at risk
- patch things up
- bestowed
- comply with
- dispense with
- threaten
- do the same in return
- make the best of

1. jeopardize ____________________
2. undermine ____________________
3. extrapolate ____________________
4. reciprocate ____________________
5. conform ____________________
6. waive ____________________
7. advocate ____________________
8. reconcile ____________________
9. emulate ____________________
10. reconcile ____________________

**F.** Complete each sentence to show that you understand the meaning of the underlined word.

1. Michael wished his parents would waive their ______________________________

______________________________________________________________.

2. Ann reciprocated the gift of money from her grandmother by ____________________

______________________________________________________________.

3. A quality of her friend Caroline that Hope wishes to emulate is __________________

______________________________________________________________.

4. Shane's hopes to become quarterback of the football team were undermined when ______

______________________________________________________________.

5. One possible negative consequence of always trying to conform to one's peers is _______

______________________________________________________________.

6. Ned jeopardized his chances of getting a summer job at Disneyland by ______________

______________________________________________________________.

7. Rachel and Casey extrapolated about the outcome of their debate about gun control with the comment, "____________________________________________________

______________________________________________________________."

8. In their debate, Rachel and Casey advocated ______________________________

______________________________________________________________.

9. Emmalin and Becky reconciled after ______________________________________

______________________________________________________________.

10. Even though he was not happy about it, Casey was reconciled to __________________

______________________________________________________________.

# Vocabulary List 16
## Vivacious Verbs

| **Word**<br>[pronunciation]<br>**other word form** | **Definition**<br>• sample sentence |
|---|---|
|  |  |
| **allege**<br>[uh LEJ]<br>**allegation** (n) | to claim that something is true without proof<br>• The man alleged that he saw a UFO flying above the desert. |
| **amplify**<br>[AM pluh fy]<br>**amplification** (n) | to make sounds louder<br>• The speaker requested a microphone to amplify his voice. |
| **censure**<br>[SEN shur] | express severe disapproval of someone or something<br>• The student was censured for plagiarizing his research paper. |
| **divulge**<br>[dih VULJ]<br>**divulgence** (n) | to reveal private or sensitive information<br>• He was hesitant to divulge his birthplace. |
| **epitomize**<br>[eh PIT uh miyz]<br>**epitome** (n) | to be a perfect example of something<br>• The charming woman epitomized sophistication. |
| **instigate**<br>[IN stih geyt]<br>**instigator** (n)<br>**instigation** (n) | to cause or motivate an action or event<br>• The policy change was instigated by citizens unhappy with current tax rates. |
| **posit**<br>[POZ it]<br>**position** (n) | to put forward an idea or theory as the basis of argument or discussion<br>• The scientist posited that climate change was in part caused by human activity. |
| **prioritize**<br>[pri AWR uh tiyz]<br>**priority** (n) | to designate or treat something as more important than other things<br>• She prioritized which of her bills needed to be paid first. |
| **validate**<br>[VAL ih deyt]<br>**validation** (n) | to confirm the worthiness or legitimacy of something<br>• The audience validated their enjoyment of the play by standing and giving sustained applause. |

**A.** Write the best list word that the synonyms, idioms, or phrases define to complete each sentence.

| | | | |
|---|---|---|---|
| prioritized | divulged | posited | alleged |
| amplify | epitomizes | validated | defer |
| censure | instigated | | |

1. Ann ______________________ healthy eating and exercise so she could stay in shape for swim team.

   ranked put first focus on hierarchized

2. For his birthday, Ned's dad gave him a gift certificate so he could purchase a device to ______________________ the sound of his acoustic guitar through loudspeakers.

   intensify increase boost turn up

3. In the Greek myth of Daedalus and Icarus, after watching birds fly, Daedalus ______________________ that he could make wings out of bird feathers and fly to freedom.

   hypothesized proposed asserted postulated

4. The IACHR (Inter-American Commission on Human Rights) gives countries the right and duty to ______________________ those responsible for human rights violations.

   condemn denounce rebuke chastise

5. Heidi ______________________ Emmalin's anger when she said, "You've got the right to be angry about the rude way she talked to you."

   proved substantiated corroborated verified

6. Because of the high price and the scarcity of bread, Parisian women were ______________________ to march on Versailles in 1789 to confront Louis XVI.

   influenced spurred-on incited motivated

7. Robert Mueller and his committee investigated the ______________________ Russian interference in the 2016 election and collusion with the Trump campaign.

   asserted contended accused stated

8. His class was shocked when Mr. Clark ______________________ that he received D's in history when he was a high school student.

   disclosed admitted declared spilled the beans

9. Mr. Clark's revelation of his prior poor grades in history was surprising because now he ______________________ a knowledgeable and creative teacher of social studies.

   embodies represents exemplifies typifies

**B.** Write the best word from the choice box to complete each sentence.

| | | | |
|---|---|---|---|
| validation | extrapolate | divulgence | instigator |
| censured | epitome | position | amplification |
| allegation | instigation | priority | |

1. For her persuasive speech, Emmalin plans to support the _______________ that using the electoral college vote instead of the popular vote to elect a president is unfair.

2. After Piper made the _______________ that her younger brother Charlie took her diary, she was later embarrassed when she found it in the closet under a pile of clothes.

3. Principal Zhang purchased a wireless microphone system with four handheld microphones for sound _______________ of debates and panel discussions.

4. Harvey said that he makes it a/an _______________ to do his most difficult homework assignment first.

5. Christina promised that _______________ of the secret that Hannah shared with her would never happen.

6. Luke was the _______________of a typical bully because teasing and picking on others seemed to make him feel more powerful and important.

7. The terrible smell coming from the boys' locker room was the _______________ for a search by the janitor of every locker.

8. The class unanimously gave _______________ to Gary for his repertoire of good card tricks.

9. Ms. Cosgrove _______________ any words or actions that did not show good sportsmanship in gym class.

10. Leonardo DaVinci, an inventor ahead of his time, was the _______________ of ideas such as a flying machine and an anemometer to measure wind speed.

### C. Story Challenge

Write the best word from the choice box to fill each blank in the story.

| | | | |
|---|---|---|---|
| allege | censured | epitomized | instigate |
| posit | divulging | jeopardize | validate |
| amplify | prioritize | | |

## "To Be or Not to Be" – The Art of Persuasion

When her writing students were seated, Ms. Paterson made an announcement. "At the school board meeting, a six-day school week was approved. Consequently, this policy will go into effect for the next semester, which begins in January," she clarified.

The class reacted with boos, jeers, and catcalls. When their responses reached a near revolutionary pitch, Ms. Paterson said that she was just joking with them to (1)____________________ a reaction. "Obviously, my opening to today's lesson on persuasion shows the value of a shocking or surprising anecdote to begin a speech," she laughed.

"Persuasion is the art of getting others to do what you want them to do," Ms. Paterson began. "Patrick Henry (2)____________________ the power of persuasion when he used his persuasive speaking skills to rouse the colonists to action to prepare an army to fight the British."

"When Patrick Henry wrote, 'The summer soldier and the sunshine patriot will, in this crisis, shrink from the service of his country,' Henry (3)____________________ those colonists who supported the thought of revolution when the idea was simply words, but who recoiled when it was time for action," Ms. Paterson explained.

"Three persuasive strategies are <u>pathos</u>, <u>logos</u>, and <u>ethos</u>," Ms. Paterson said. "Pathos is an appeal to emotions such as sadness, fear, and guilt. Patrick Henry was using pathos with his statement, making the colonists feel guilty if they didn't actively support the war," Ms. Paterson explained.

"Logos is an appeal to logic or reason. When the persuasive speaker uses evidence and statistics to support his or her claims, he or she is using logos. When the evidence comes from a credible source, the speaker or writer is using ethos by showing that the source is reliable and in sync with the principles or ethics of the time period," Ms. Paterson continued.

Next, Ms. Paterson passed out pocket copies of the Constitution of the United States. "I'm sure you all recall that the U.S. Constitution is the fundamental law of the United States, and that it is a document that was written by a group of 55 men known as The Framers in 1787. In addition to the Bill of Rights, there are 7 Articles in the Constitution, and each article has many sections. Additionally, there are 27 Amendments that have been added to the Constitution through the years.

"Ms. Paterson, I thought we were going to learn about persuasion, so why do we need a copy of the Constitution?" asked Luke.

"There is a connection, Luke," said Ms. Paterson. "This will be your persuasive assignment."

> Imagine that you are a U.S. senator who believes strongly that a change is needed in the Constitution. Write a speech in which you will try to persuade your fellow senators to vote for the change you suggest.

"Mr. Clark, your history teacher, is aware of the persuasive assignment and will discuss the way changes can be made to the Constitution. Ms. Palmer, on the other hand, in speech class will go over public speaking skills important in persuasion."

"The prewriting process is of the utmost importance in persuasive writing," emphasized Ms. Paterson. "The first step is to choose your issue, in this case, a change you would like to see in the Constitution. You might (4)____________________________ that a president should be elected directly by the people, rather than by the Electoral College. Or perhaps you might (5)____________________________ that capital punishment should be abolished in all states. Remember to first do some research to get an idea of some controversial constitutional issues."

"Once you've chosen your issue, and you've done adequate research and reading about your issue, it's time to brainstorm your reasons for advocating change. Then the fun begins—you gather evidence that supports your reasons for change. At this point, the Internet and library will be your best friends. Facts, examples, anecdotes, observations, and authoritative opinions are among the kinds of evidence you can use." Ms. Paterson noted, "Remember that the very first information you need to find is the status-quo of your issue. Can anyone explain this and give an example?"

Rachel raised her hand. “The status-quo means the existing situation—what’s happening currently. For example, if I was arguing for ending capital punishment in all U.S. states, I would need to find out which states still use capital punishment, and which states have abolished the death penalty.”

“Excellent, Rachel. Also, remember ‘ethos’ in your evidence-gathering. All your sources should be credible and reliable, and you will need to (6)__________________________ the credibility as you speak. You don’t want to make the mistake of (7)________________________ information until you have done a thorough job of fact-checking and making sure your sources are unbiased and credible,” she reminded.

“As you gather evidence,” Ms. Paterson continued, (8)________________________ your support to make it clear which of your reasons for change are the most important.”

“Additionally, as you gather evidence, consider what the counter-arguments will be. What would someone who disagrees with you say? You also need evidence to counter any objections to your arguments.”

“Ms. Palmer will discuss speech delivery skills, such as the need to (9)_________________________ your voice and speak in a way that shows confidence in your argumentation. Tomorrow, I will give you an outline for your persuasive speech, and then you will have two weeks to work diligently. Have a great day!” Ms. Paterson said as class ended.

Persuasive Appeals

- pathos - emotions
- logos – logic or reason
- ethos – consistent with current morals or ethics

**D.** The underlined part in each sentence is a synonym, idiom, phrase, or definition for a list word. Unscramble the list word and write the word on the blank.

1. All of Dylan's friends promised not to reveal the plans for his surprise birthday party. _______________ ueldvig

2. Ned proposed the idea that students would be more awake and alert if school started an hour later in the morning. _______________ sitoedp

3. Most of the demonstrators were peaceful and law-abiding; however, some gathered just to cause trouble. _______________ gnteisita

4. A doctor's stethoscope increases the sound of a beating human heart. _______________ lieaimsfp

5. Ms. Palmer instructed her journalism students about the importance of knowing the legitimacy of the information they intend to report. _______________ andlivtiga

6. Bullying was emphatically disapproved of in or outside of school. _______________ uecdrens

7. The defense attorney claimed that his client was innocent. _______________ elegald

8. Notre Dame Cathedral in Paris, France, is a perfect example of French Gothic architecture. _______________ temeiposiz

9. When Suzanne ranked her New Year's resolutions, she decided that practicing piano each day was the most important. _______________ tieripdozir

**E.** Write the word, idiom, or phrase from the choice box that best defines each list word.

- to claim
- increase loudness
- express strong disapproval
- disclose
- exemplify
- motivate
- hypothesize
- categorize
- verify
- comply with

1. prioritize ______________________
2. epitomize ______________________
3. allege ______________________
4. posit ______________________
5. amplify ______________________
6. censure ______________________
7. divulge ______________________
8. validate ______________________
9. instigate ______________________

**F.** Complete each sentence to show that you understand the meaning of the underlined word.

1. Ms. Paterson's journal prompt asked the students to <u>prioritize</u> their responsibilities and Aiden listed the following as his top three: ________________________________________________.

2. Two devices that can <u>amplify</u> the human voice are ________________________________________________.

3. Mr. Clark said that a presidential candidate should be expected to <u>divulge</u> ________________________________________________.

4. Caroline <u>epitomizes</u> ________________________________________________ because ________________________________________________.

5. Kara seemed to like to <u>instigate</u> ________________________________________________.

6. He needed a lawyer when it was <u>alleged</u> that he ________________________________________________.

7. For her science experiment, Suzanne began by <u>positing</u> that ________________________________________________.

8. A good way to <u>validate</u> an accomplishment of a friend or relative would be to ________________________________________________.

9. Some actions that are <u>censured</u> in Milly's family are ________________________________________________.

 

# Review: Lists 13-16

**A.** Use the clues to complete the crossword puzzle with vocabulary words, synonyms, or information from the activities.

**Across**

1. A synonym for euphonious
2. Reveals
4. Extrapolate
6. Support
7. Force
8. Strong disapproval
9. Small offense
13. A heavy book
14. Emulate

**Down**

1. Opinion that cannot be disputed
3. Damage
5. Waive
9. Succinct
10. Poise
11. Jurisprudence expert
12. Conform

**B.** Circle the answer which best completes the sentence.

1. Something that needs to be **validated** is
   a. a passport.
   b. a pet dog or cat.
   c. a good friend.

2. A **caustic** remark might be described as
   a. unusual.
   b. thoughtful.
   c. cutting.

3. One could **prioritize** a
   a. popular song.
   b. list of tasks.
   c. hot-fudge sundae.

4. Something described as **verdant** would be this color
   a. purple.
   b. black.
   c. green.

5. Which of the following would not be used to **amplify**
   a. binoculars.
   b. a hearing aid.
   c. a megaphone.

6. To **posit** means to
   a. to put forth a theory.
   b. to lend a piece of note paper.
   c. to post a Facebook message.

7. **Ambivalent** could be best used to describe
   a. new high-rise buildings.
   b. feelings.
   c. Grand Canyon photos.

8. A **cursory** look would not be sufficient for
   a. a fire hazard inspection.
   b. looking at books in a bookstore.
   c. checking Internet articles.

9. A **caustic** substance might be
   a. used as a hand lotion.
   b. added to the cake mix.
   c. kept away from children.

10. For **contemptible** behavior, one might
    a. receive a trophy.
    b. be scorned.
    c. need a good night's sleep.

11. One should **reciprocate** when
    a. receiving a gift.
    b. in the shower.
    c. studying for a quiz.

12. An antonym for **discord** might be
    a. strife.
    b. harmony.
    c. conflict.

13. A quality of an **interlocutor** is
    a. shyness.
    b. greediness.
    c. talkativeness.

14. A **parasite** might be one
    a. who often borrows things.
    b. who gives you a gift.
    c. with whom you play chess.

**C.** Write the best word that might be included in the news story for each headline.

| | | |
|---|---|---|
| fait accompli | didactic | parasite |
| instigate | alleged | caustic |
| jeopardize | emulate | epitome |
| reconcile | empathetic | |

1. ______________________ "Prehistoric Artifact Suspected to Be From Sumerian Era"

2. ______________________ "Comedian's Sarcasm Offends Politicians at the Annual Press Banquet"

3. ______________________ "Dictator's Actions Provoke Rebellion"

4. ______________________ "Local Churches Open Doors to Immigrants"

5. ______________________ "Budget Plan Is Passed After Approval by Majority of Congress"

6. ______________________ "Organism Discovered That Causes Ebola"

7. ______________________ "A Diet High in Saturated Fat and Sugar Puts Health at Risk"

8. ______________________ "Fans Copy Star Wars Characters' Costumes At Annual Convention"

9. ______________________ "South African President De Klerk and Nelson Mandela Reach Agreement That Will Lead to the End of Apartheid"

10. ______________________ "New Players Nominated for Baseball Hall of Fame"

 

# Vocabulary List 17
## Astute Adjectives

| **Word**<br>[pronunciation]<br>**other word form**<br> | **Definition**<br>• sample sentence<br> |
|---|---|
| **authentic**<br>[aw THEN tik]<br>**authenticity** (n) | real or genuine<br>• Mr. Clark showed his history class <u>authentic</u> posters from WWII. |
| **didactic**<br>[diy DAK tik] | intended for instruction<br>• Mrs. Bradley has a <u>didactic</u> set of books about famous scientists in her classroom. |
| **dilatory**<br>[DIL uh tawr ee] | tending to delay or procrastinate<br>• One of the <u>dilatory</u> tactics used by the Senate to avoid a vote on a bill is a filibuster. |
| **incendiary**<br>[in SEN dee er ee] | [1]a substance or device designed to explode or cause fires<br>[2]actions or words that incite discontent or anger<br>• [1]Buried <u>incendiary</u> land mines were a danger to the troops in Afghanistan.<br>• [2]The politician's <u>incendiary</u> words about immigrants prompted protests everywhere. |
| **nefarious**<br>[neh FAIR ee uhs] | extremely wicked, evil, or immoral<br>• Students learned about the <u>nefarious</u> actions of the Mafia in the early 20th century. |
| **palatable**<br>[PAL ah tuh buhl] | pleasant to the taste<br>• The French food at the Bistro de Louisa was very <u>palatable</u>. |
| **perpetual**<br>[per PECH oo uhl]<br>**perpetuity** (n) | continuing forever<br>• Sadly, war seems to be a <u>perpetual</u> condition in the human race. |
| **petulant**<br>[PECH uh luhnt]<br>**petulance** (n) | childishly angry, annoyed, or bad-tempered<br>• Becky's little brother Charlie became <u>petulant</u> when he didn't get his way. |
| **quixotic**<br>[kwik SOT ik] | idealistic, impractical ideas or plans that usually do not succeed<br>• "Unless you work diligently in school, the chances of someday attending a college of your choice may be <u>quixotic</u>," advised Principal Zhang. |

**A.** Write the best list word that the synonyms, idioms, or phrases define to complete each sentence.

| | | | |
|---|---|---|---|
| quixotic | dilatory | palatable | perpetual |
| authentic | incendiary | petulant | dogmatic |
| didactic | nefarious | incendiary | |

1. The goalie's ________________________ movements allowed opponents to score the first point in the soccer game.

   dawdling lagging sluggish unhurried

2. Protesters gathered when the ________________________ white supremacist scheduled a rally to speak on the college campus.

   seditious rabble-rousing subversive controversial

3. Brendan's jealous girlfriend usually has a/an ________________________ outburst when Brendan simply talks to another girl.

   pouting peevish whiny querulous

4. "You are a/an ________________________ procrastinator and your dilatory ways must change," demanded Michael's father.

   incessant endless interminable eternal

5. Wonder Woman fights evildoers and stops ________________________ villains such as Ares, Cheetah, Doctor Poison, and Circe.

   iniquitous villainous wicked despicable

6. Many believe that establishing world peace is a/an ________________________ idea.

   chimerical utopian starry-eyed unrealistic

7. Celeste likes historical fiction because books such as Steinbeck's *The Grapes of Wrath* are entertaining as well as ________________________.

   academic educational informative pedagogic

8. Max's grandmother purchased a/an ________________________ Picasso sketch at a Sotheby's art auction in London, England.

   bona fide verifiable original true

9. On July 4, Americans enjoy patriotic parties and dazzling displays of ________________________ fireworks.

   combustible flammable ignitable burnable

10. Trying to reduce her family's salt intake and still serve ________________________ food, Hillary's mom uses different herbs and spices such as ginger, basil, and cardamom.

    appetizing flavorful tasty delicious

**B.** Write the best word from the choice box to completе each sentence.

| | | | |
|---|---|---|---|
| dilatory | prehensile | quixotic | incendiary |
| incendiary | perpetuity | didactic | palatable |
| petulance | nefarious | authenticity | |

1. In 1775, Patrick Henry gave a/an ________________________ speech at the meeting of the Second Virginia Convention, urging the formation of a militia to fight against Great Britain.

2. The word _________________________ is derived from an early 17th century novel by Miguel de Cervantes about an elderly man, inspired by chivalrous knights, who sets out to undo the wrongs he sees in the modern world and fails in his quests.

3. Brendan's _________________________ was the result of Suzanne's refusal to let him use her iPad at lunch time.

4. A flame burns in ________________________ at the gravesite in Arlington National Cemetery of U.S. President John F. Kennedy.

5. The ______________________ of the documents in the National Archives, such as the *Constitution of the United States*, has been validated by experts.

6. "Harvey, your work is usually carefully completed and quite good, but your ________________________ habit of turning in assignments after deadlines results in lower grades," warned Mrs. Cole.

7. Mrs. Bradley encourages group discussions in her science class, unlike Mr. Clark who is more ______________________ and lectures in history class while the students take notes.

8. "I know that using my mom's laptop computer without asking was wrong, but it was not exactly _______________________ behavior," complained Justin after his mom grounded him for a week even after he apologized.

9. ______________________ delicacies such as German potato salad, Mexican empanadas, Chinese spring rolls, and Indian chicken curry were served at the International Buffet.

10. Greek Fire, Flaming Arrows, and Molotov Cocktails were __________________________ devices used in warfare in history.

### C. Story Challenge

Write the best word from the choice box to fill each blank in the story.

| | | | |
|---|---|---|---|
| authentic | dilatory | quixotic | perpetual |
| didactic | palatable | incendiary | petulant |
| euphonious | nefarious | | |

## Persuasion Moves to Speech Class

To surprise Ms. Palmer on her birthday, Christina provided a tray of (1)__________________________ treats—her famous oatmeal raisin cookies—that she passed to the class.

"Thank you, Christina, for the wonderful treat and all of you for your cards and birthday wishes. It is tempting to be (2)_______________________ and put off today's work, but I promised Ms. Paterson that I would review the process of composing and delivering a persuasive speech."

"Your first task," Ms. Palmer began, "is to grab the audience's attention. A startling statement, rhetorical question, quotation, dramatic story, or photograph or other visual aid are all good methods of hooking the audience."

Becky told Ms. Palmer about Ms. Paterson's startling statement (in composition class) about a six-day school week that was (3)__________________________ and definitely got an angry response from the class. "Such a startling statement would certainly grab attention," laughed Ms. Palmer.

"Next, you must establish a need," she continued. "You must show your audience that a problem exists and that there is a need to change. To do this you must be (4)_____________________________ and teach your audience about the extent of the problem—the status quo. If you expect to be believed, you must support all of your information such as facts, figures, graphs, diagrams, and expert witness testimony by citing reliable sources."

"For example, I might say, 'Robert Preidt, a journalist for CBS News, stated in a February 2016, news broadcast that compared to 22 other high-income nations, the United States gun-related murder rate is 25 times higher,' in a persuasive essay." Ms. Palmer continued, "You can report your sources at the end of your persuasive paper in Works Cited; however, in a speech you need to verbally cite your sources."

Ms. Palmer went on to say, "Your next task is to outline a solution to the problem. Your solution must be (5)________________________, not (6)__________________________. The audience must believe that your solution can actually solve the problem. Your assignment from Ms. Paterson is to show ways that you think the Constitution or an amendment to the Constitution should be changed and can be changed—to show that times change and what was written in the 1700s does not need to be (7)________________________. Think of this as the satisfaction step. Again you must thoroughly support your solution to show its effectiveness with credible facts and figures."

Ms. Palmer continued, "Following your plan, you must acknowledge that there are those who would oppose your change and disagree with you. Now you must offer counter arguments. In order to do this effectively, you must have thoroughly researched your topic to discover these opposing arguments. For example, if you were arguing for stricter gun control and your opponent states that criminals with (8)________________________ intent will always circumvent any legislation and acquire firearms anyway, you must be prepared with an argument to counter your opponent's argument."

"Visualization is next," explained Ms. Palmer. "You must show your audience how they will benefit from your solution. Again, support is needed. Possibly examples could be used that show where your plan worked in another place."

"Finally, end your speech by calling your audience to action. What can they do to help make the changes that you propose?" Ms. Palmer reminded.

"Once you have your speech composed, it is time to consider an effective delivery. Your goal is to appear convincing and confident. To do this you must have good posture, be dressed professionally, and speak in a strong voice. Remember to speak slowly and to use effective pauses and emphasis where they are appropriate. And of course, eye contact with all of the members of your audience is very important."

"I plan to come to Ms. Paterson's class to listen to your persuasive speeches," said Ms. Palmer as class ended.

Luke left class in a/an (9)________________________ mood, less concerned about his persuasive speech then the fact that Christina wouldn't give him the three cookies that were left on the plate.

### Steps in Composing a Persuasive Speech

1. grab attention
2. prove a problem exists
3. establish a need for change
4. present a solution to the problem
5. prove that the solution would work
6. address counter arguments
7. visualize the solution
8. call audience to action

**D.** The underlined part in each sentence is a synonym, idiom, phrase, or definition for a list word. Unscramble the list word and write the word on the blank.

1. A melodrama was a Victorian drama with stereotypical characters such as a <u>wicked</u> landlord and a sweet, young naïve tenant. ____________ sonfueair

2. The imposition of unfair taxes on the American colonists by Great Britain was an action that caused <u>provocative</u> feelings, moving the colonists closer to revolution. ____________ daiycinrne

3. Her wish for world peace is admirable but <u>not practical</u> at this time. ____________ otiuciqx

4. <u>Explosive</u> substances such as fireworks or ammunition are forbidden on airplanes. ____________ cdrneiyain

5. The smell of brownies baking was an <u>appetizing</u> temptation. ____________ leatlapab

6. Cindy often became <u>crabby</u> when things didn't go her way. ____________ utnlatep

7. Mr. Clark showed his students a/an <u>instructional</u> film about Mahatma Gandhi when they were studying India during the time when the country was under British rule. ____________ tcadiidc

8. Piper's little brother, Charlie, seems to always be in <u>endless</u> motion, never sitting still for a moment. ____________ tpelurpae

9. "My great-grandpa has a <u>genuine</u> first edition copy of the book *Gone With the Wind* published in 1936," said Justin. ____________ ntactuhie

10. Hannah was <u>tardy</u> in sending in her application for a summer job at the veterinarian clinic, so consequently, someone else was hired. ____________ oiaylrdt

**E.** Write the word, idiom, or phrase from the choice box that best defines each list word.

- trustworthy
- evil
- unrealistic
- tasty
- embryonic
- combustible
- rousing
- peevish
- lagging
- forever
- instructive

1. nefarious ______________________

2. incendiary ______________________

3. palatable ______________________

4. perpetual ______________________

5. authentic ______________________

6. dilatory ______________________

7. quixotic ______________________

8. incendiary ______________________

9. didactic ______________________

10. petulant ______________________

**F.** Complete each sentence to show that you understand the meaning of the underlined word.

1. Milly wished for an authentic ______________________________________________

_______________________________________________________________________.

2. "That's a quixotic idea," Becky said when Julia _________________________________

_______________________________________________________________________.

3. Christopher said an incendiary device is in his home and its purpose is ______________

_______________________________________________________________________.

4. Mrs. Bradley's science students watched a didactic documentary on the subject of ______

_______________________________________________________________________.

5. A nefarious person who Mr. Clark talked about in history class was ____________ who

_______________________________________________________________________.

6. In history, an incendiary action or incendiary words that caused anger or revolt was

_______________________________________________________________________.

7. Suzanne acted petulant person when she_________________________________________

_______________________________________________________________________.

8. Gary's habit of being dilatory about ___________________________________________

resulted in ____________________________________________________________.

9. Three of Ned's favorite palatable treats are_______________________________________

_______________________________________________________________________.

10. The word perpetual makes Principal Zhang think of ____________________________

_______________________________________________________________________.

# Vocabulary List 18
## Vexing Verbs

| **Word**<br>[pronunciation]<br>**other word form** | **Definition**<br>• sample sentence |
|---|---|
|  |  |
| **absolve**<br>[ab ZOLV]<br>**absolution** (n) | to free from blame, guilt, or responsibility<br>• The suspect had an alibi and was absolved of guilt. |
| **coalesce**<br>[koh uh LES]<br>**coalescence** (n) | to come together to form one mass or whole<br>• A small group of patriots coalesced, demanding freedom. |
| **curtail**<br>[ker TEYL]<br>**curtailment** (n) | to reduce, limit, or stop something<br>• To curtail littering, reminder signs were posted along the freeway. |
| **debilitate**<br>[dih BIHL ih teyt]<br>**debilitation** (n) | to become physically or mentally weakened<br>• Even though the elderly man was debilitated, he still took daily walks using a walker. |
| **dissipate**<br>[DIS uh peyt]<br>**dissipation** (n) | to disappear or to stop existing or happening<br>• He freely spent the money he received from an inheritance and it soon dissipated. |
| **espouse**<br>[eh SPOUZ]<br>**espousal** (n) | to give support to an idea, principle, cause, or belief<br>• Principal Zhang espoused the idea of having a school choir. |
| **relinquish**<br>[rih LING kwish]<br>**relinquishment** (n) | to part with a possession or right<br>• Shane relinquished his bedroom to his Aunt Margaret when she was visiting. |
| **repudiate**<br>[ree PYOO dee eyt]<br>**repudiation** (n) | to refuse to acknowledge, ratify, or recognize<br>• Some senators repudiated the president's choice for Secretary of State. |
| **vacillate**<br>[VAS uh leyt]<br>**vacillation** (n) | to waver between conflicting positions or courses of action<br>• Hannah's sister vacillated between going to Stanford or UC Berkeley to college. |

**A.** Write the best list word that the synonyms, idioms, or phrases define to complete each sentence.

| absolve | curtail | repudiated | debilitated |
|---|---|---|---|
| relinquish | dissipated | vacillated | posit |
| coalesced | espoused | | |

1. Michael ________________________ his father's charge that he was a procrastinator by reminding him of his excellent grades and his part-time job.

   renounced denied rebutted brushed aside

2. Interested students ______________________ to form a debate club after it was approved by the administration and Ms. Palmer agreed to be the advisor.

   merged united combined blended

3. Suzanne ________________________ between joining the tennis team or the soccer team because she played and enjoyed both sports.

   hesitated wavered fluctuated dithered

4. The lawyer was determined to appeal the verdict in order to __________his client of guilt.

   exonerate pardon vindicate release

5. Children who are _____________________ with life-threatening illnesses are given the joy and hope of seeing a wish come true by the Make-A-Wish Foundation.

   enervated incapacitated sapped enfeebled

6. Environmentalists hope that electric cars will help to ______________________ pollution, especially in big cities.

   cut decrease restrict curb

7. Milly's hopes of getting an A on the science test ______________________ when she couldn't remember all of the elements in the periodic table.

   vanished evaporated dispersed scattered

8. Mahatma Gandhi ___________________________ the idea that eliminating world poverty must be a priority when he said, "Poverty is the worst form of violence."

   adopted promoted championed advocated

9. In Tibet, when a child is identified as the new Dalai Lama, the parents __________________________ him to be raised by Buddhist monks.

   give up leave cede surrender

 

**B.** Write the best word from the choice box to complete each sentence.

| repudiation | allegation | dissipation | absolution |
|---|---|---|---|
| relinquishment | coalescence | curtailment | vacillation |
| debilitation | espousal | | |

1. Casey's ________________________ in choosing a subject for his narrative essay finally ended when he decided to write about a family trip to Bryce Canyon National Park in Utah.

2. "Following taking notes from a plethora of sources, the next step is the ________________________ of all your information into an organized research essay," advised Ms. Paterson.

3. "I hope my ________________________ of Brendan for class president helps him win," declared Mandy.

4. Michael received ________________________ for leaving the hamster cage door open when he found "Checkers" under his sister's bed.

5. Dylan recalled a time of ________________________ after a fall from his bike resulted in a cast on his broken leg, and the challenge of hobbling around on crutches for three months.

6. "Math test time," reminded Mr. Salter. "Time for ______________________ of all chit-chat."

7. ____________________________ of the smoke smell took almost two weeks after the small fire in the school kitchen.

8. Her friends defended Mandy with a/an ________________________ of the charge that she was arrogant and a show-off.

9. __________________________ of the rotating trophy to the Warren Bears when the soccer team lost in the finals, made the team determined to get it back the following season.

### C. Story Challenge

Write the best word from the choice box to fill each blank in the story.

| | | | |
|---|---|---|---|
| absolve | debilitated | espousing | repudiates |
| coalesce | amplify | relinquish | vacillated |
| curtailed | dissipate | | |

## Persuasive Speeches Begin

Some of the students had (1)________________________ when it was time to choose a topic for their persuasive speech. "Indecision is not an excuse," said Ms. Paterson. "I will not (2)______________________ anyone for not being prepared on time," she added.

Kara knew exactly what her speech would be about. Ever since second grade when she learned that she was not eligible to be the U.S. President, she was very bothered by this idea.

Kara had been born in Marseille, France. Her parents were French citizens when Kara was born. Since that time, Kara and her parents had become naturalized citizens of the United States. A naturalized citizen is one who was born in another country but had lawfully become a citizen of the United States. A naturalized citizen has all the rights of a natural born citizen, but an attempt to become president or vice president of the United States would be (3)__________________________.

This was a definite problem for Kara, who did not wish to (4)____________________ the possibility that she could someday be the U.S. President. Therefore, Kara decided to focus her persuasive speech on (5)_________________________ a change to Article II, Section I, of the Constitution. That article states the following: "No person except a natural born citizen, or a citizen of the United States, at the time of the adoption of this Constitution, shall be eligible to the office of President..."

Kara began her speech with an anecdotal hook: "Madeleine Jean Albright, a gifted politician and diplomat and the first woman to be the United States Secretary of State, could never have hoped to be the U.S. President. Why? She had been born in Czechoslovakia of Czech parents."

Next, Kara stated her position that the Article II, Section I, of the Constitution should be changed. She said that the U.S. is (6)__________________________ by Article II, Section I, because there are more than 12.8 million naturalized citizens in the U.S. and certainly some of these naturalized citizens, such as Madeleine Albright, would be highly qualified to be U.S. President.

"The natural born citizen clause (7)__________________________ a central principle of American democracy that all citizens have equal rights," she argued. "This clause does not omit naturalized citizens." She continued by showing that the original "natural born citizen clause" is no longer relevant.

"In the 1700s, the Founding Fathers added the clause so no foreign prince could buy his way into the presidency." Kara continued by explaining that this is not the case today and that naturalized citizens are very loyal to the U.S. She also added that the judgment of the American people in elections would keep disloyal people from being elected.

As a solution to the problem, Kara proposed changing the wording of Article II, Section I to the following: "A person shall be eligible for the office of president if he or she has been a citizen or a naturalized citizen of the United States for a period of fourteen years and has attained the age of thirty-five."

Kara said that those who disagreed might say that a naturalized citizen might show favoritism to his or her place of birth. "Opponents of changing the constitution might also say that the attachment of the president to the U.S. must be absolute, and this attachment can only come from being born in, educated in, and formed in this country with no allegiance to another country," explained Kara.

"To counter opponent's arguments, education is the answer," said Kara. "If the American people learn about the loyalty and dedication to the U.S. by naturalized citizens and became knowledgeable about the many qualified naturalized citizens for U.S. President, they might (8)__________________________ around the idea of changing the clause."

"Imagine a baby born in a foreign country and adopted by American parents. Think about how demoralizing it is to him or her when learning in school that he or she cannot run for president some day."

"Back to equal rights," said Kara. "Again, this natural born citizen clause violates the equal rights guaranteed by the Constitution and the Equal Protection Clause of the 14th Amendment. The Equal Protection Clause was originally added to prevent segregation as a form of discrimination based on skin color, but discrimination because of national origin is also a form of segregation. Additionally, the 15th and 19th Amendments have been added to protect the rights of women and of racial and ethnic minorities. Now it's time to protect the rights of naturalized citizens," Kara emphatically stated.

"I urge you to write letters to your Congressmen and women to encourage them to consider changing this Article of the Constitution. Thank you for listening, and my hopes will not (9)____________________________. I hope someday to be your United States President," Kara emphatically concluded.

Requirements to be U.S. President
U.S. Constitution, Article II, Section 1

- must be a natural born citizen of the U.S.
- must be at least 35 years old
- must have lived in the country for the last 14 years

**D.** The underlined part in each sentence is a synonym, idiom, phrase, or definition for a list word. Unscramble the list word and write the word on the blank.

1. Celeste rejected the idea that she was selfish and said she was generous, except to those who consistently wanted to borrow school supplies. ____________ tudaedrepi

2. Casey freed Tim from all guilt for accidentally dropping and breaking his calculator when Tim gave him money to buy a new one. ____________ odevbsal

3. *The Federalist Papers*, a collection of articles and essays that supported the U.S. Constitution was written by Alexander Hamilton, James Madison, and John Jay and published in 1788. ____________ speoedsu

4. The hopes of the Jefferson Cougar soccer team for a comeback vanished when the Livonia Lions made a goal in the last minute of the game. ____________ iestpdaisd

5. When Rachel broke her leg she had to temporarily give up her position on the cheerleading squad. ____________ lsihinrque

6. Mrs. Berkabile stopped the laughing and chatting of a group of students in the library by reminding them to respect the others who were there. ____________ iutlecrda

7. Before Hope and Harvey got a dog, they wavered between wanting a Labrador retriever or a border collie. ____________ ecliadvlta

8. Although Rachel was physically weakened by her broken leg, she joined the chess club to stay busy while her leg mended. ____________ tieditaldeb

9. Many of the Jefferson students came together to form a new club with the intent of becoming involved in community service projects. ____________ lesacdoce

**E.** Write the word, idiom, or phrase from the choice box that best defines each list word.

- hesitate
- disclaimed
- hand over
- support
- disappear
- motivate
- weaken
- reduce
- unite
- exonerate
- reject

1. repudiate ______________________
2. debilitate ______________________
3. dissipate ______________________
4. espouse ______________________
5. vacillate ______________________
6. coalesce ______________________
7. absolve ______________________
8. relinquish ______________________
9. curtail ______________________

**F.** Complete each sentence to show that you understand the meaning of the underlined word.

1. To curtail socializing and loud talking in the library, Mrs. Berkabile ____________________
_________________________________________________________________________.

2. A friend of Dylan's was debilitated when ________________________________________
_________________________________________________________________________.

3. Casey was absolved from an accusation of cheating when __________________________
_________________________________________________________________________.

4. A suggestion that Cindy would emphatically repudiate would be _____________________
_________________________________________________________________________.

5. Mandy coalesces with friends to _______________________________________________
_________________________________________________________________________.

6. A decision Hope vacillated about was___________________________________________
_________________________________________________________________________.

7. Responding to the following journal prompt, "Two things that might dissipate in fifty years," Harvey wrote about ___________________________________________________________
_________________________________________________________________________.

8. Relinquishing his___________________________ would be a sad day for Bernie because
_________________________________________________________________________.

9. A cause that Emmalin espouses is _______________________________________________
_________________________________________________________________________.

# Vocabulary List 19
## Nifty Nouns

| **Word**<br>[pronunciation]<br>**other word form** | **Definition**<br>• sample sentence |
|---|---|
|  |  |
| **candor**<br>[KAN der]<br>**candid** (adj) | the quality of being honest and straightforward in attitude and speech<br>• The speaker talked with candor about her career as an ambassador to Saudi Arabia. |
| **caricature**<br>[KAR ih kuh chur] | a comic or grotesquely exaggerated representation of someone or something<br>• Al Hirschfeld is famous for his caricatures of American celebrities. |
| **deceit**<br>[dih SEET]<br>**deceive** (v)<br>**deceitful** (adj) | fooling someone by concealing or not telling the truth<br>• A person guilty of deceit even once is difficult to trust. |
| **larceny**<br>[LAHR suh nee] | theft of someone's personal property<br>• He was convicted of grand larceny for attempting to steal two Van Gogh paintings. |
| **premise**<br>[PREM is] | an assertion that forms the basis for a theory<br>• An example of a simple premise is "what goes up must come down." |
| **premonition**<br>[pree muh NISH uhn] | a feeling of anticipation or anxiety over a future event<br>• Because of a strong premonition of falling from a high place, Heidi chose not to ride the roller coaster. |
| **serenity**<br>[suh REN ih tee]<br>**serene** (adj) | the state of being calm and peaceful<br>• Mrs. Cole said that she finds serenity on her walks through the park. |
| **temperament**<br>[TEM per uh muhnt] | the usual attitude, personality, or behavior of a person or animal<br>• Brendan's temperament vacillates between cheerfulness and sadness. |
| **turbulence**<br>[TUHR byuh lehns]<br>**turbulent** (adj) | [1]violent or unsteady movement of air, water, or some other fluid<br>[2]characterized by unrest, disorder, or insubordination<br>• [1]On her first trip on an airplane Becky experienced violent turbulence.<br>• [2]After the dictator was toppled, a period of political turbulence followed. |

**A.** Write the best list word that the synonyms, idioms, or phrases define to complete each sentence.

| | | | |
|---|---|---|---|
| candor | premonition | larceny | serenity |
| premise | caricatures | temperament | turbulence |
| turbulence | deceit | premise | |

1. "Milly, I have a/an ________________ that your piano recital will receive a standing ovation," encouraged Piper.

   hunch suspicion intuition presentiment

2. Mandy said that her Labrador retriever, Buster, usually has a playful, friendly ________________ but when chasing a Frisbee, he is aggressive.

   personality disposition attitude nature

3. Marie Curie began with a/an ________________ and then through research and investigation made discoveries in chemistry, physics, and medicine.

   proposition hypothesis assumption idea

4. The flight attendant assured the crying child that the ________________ was as normal as the waves in the ocean.

   instability agitation disturbance disorder

5. The artist Al Hirschfeld was known for his black and white ________________ of celebrities and show business stars.

   cartoons parodies lampoons false impressions

6. The Watergate scandal in the 1970s involved a break-in of the Democratic headquarters and ________________ by Nixon's administration when they attempted to cover up their involvement.

   deception duplicity pretense guile

7. In her editorial, the journalist asserted with ________________ that both sexism and misogyny are endemic in America.

   frankness truthfulness telling it like it is bluntness

8. The Desert Botanical Garden in Phoenix, Arizona, is a place of ____________________ where the visitor can see many varieties of desert plants, as well as an annual butterfly exhibit.

   tranquility peacefulness composure contentment

9. Grand ____________________ is when something is stolen that is worth a lot of money and petty ____________________ is when the stolen item is worth little.

   robbery burglary stealing breaking and entering

10. Ethnic conflict between the Italians and Puerto Ricans erupted into ____________________ in the stage musical *West Side Story* and its film adaptation.

   chaos anarchy violence mayhem

**B.** Write the best word from the choice box to complete each sentence.

| | | | |
|---|---|---|---|
| larceny | deceitful | temperament | premise |
| turbulent | fait accompli | caricatures | deceive |
| premonitions | serene | candid | |

1. Hope has a relaxed, calm ________________________ unlike her brother Harvey, who is excitable and emotional.

2. The burglars who broke into Caroline's home when the family was on vacation were apprehended and charged with ________________________.

3. Sir Walter Scott once said, "Oh, what a tangled web we weave, when first we practice to ________________________."

4. Parks in busy cities such as Central Park in New York City are ____________________ places of calm and quiet.

5. Ms. Steinman paired her art students and instructed them to draw comic ________________________ of their partners.

6. When the controversial political candidate went to the podium, a ____________________ uproar went up from protestors holding signs and yelling insults.

7. At the Jefferson Spring Festival, Rachel, who was dressed as a fortune-teller, pretended to have ________________________ about the future as she looked into her fake crystal ball.

8. "What I appreciate about Julia," said Hannah, "is her ________________________ way of speaking—always telling the truth, even when the truth might be difficult to hear."

9. Many ancient civilizations, including Greece, believed in the ______________________ of a flat Earth.

10. The baseball player was ________________________ when he denied using performance enhancing drugs.

## C. Story Challenge

Write the best word from the choice box to fill each blank in the story.

| | | | |
|---|---|---|---|
| deceit | peccadillo | premise | turbulent |
| temperament | larceny | candor | serenity |
| premonition | caricatures | | |

### Talking About Theme

Mrs. Cole's English students had just finished reading Stephen Crane's classic novel set during the American Civil War, *The Red Badge of Courage*. "Can anyone tell me one of the themes of this novel?" she questioned.

"Easy," replied Luke. "The theme is war, because the novel is all about the Civil War."

"Luke, you've correctly identified the subject of the novel, but subject does not mean theme," she explained. "<u>Theme is an opinion expressed by the author about the subject in the novel</u>. Can anyone identify an opinion of Stephen Crane's about war after reading his story?" she asked.

"I think Crane's opinion is that war is (1)________________________, terrifying, and horrible," offered Caroline.

"Good, Caroline. You correctly identified one of the themes of the novel. Also, remember that in a novel there may be a main theme as well as additional themes. Can anyone identify another theme in Stephen Crane's novel?"

"Nature is not concerned about man's troubles," said Tim. "I remember you told us before we began reading the novel that Crane was part of the Naturalism movement in American Literature in the late 1800s and that this movement was when writers took a more realistic, factual look at nature. They looked at nature with (2)________________________ instead of with a romanticized or unrealistic view. According to the Realists and Naturalists, nature was not necessarily always a place of (3)________________________ and beauty, but could be harsh, unmerciful, and devastating."

"Tim, I think my (4)________________________ that you kids wouldn't remember our pre-reading discussion was wrong. You have given me faith that you really listen. Thank you, and you are correct. As Tim explained, one of the themes in the novel is that the universe is indifferent to human life," Mrs. Cole affirmed.

Mrs. Cole continued. "A writer presents his or her ideas through the setting, plot, and various methods of characterization. As readers, we learn through these elements how the author views human life and the way he or she believes the world works."

"Think of any fictional works that you are familiar with, including short stories, books, and movies, and identify one theme," challenged Mrs. Cole.

Aiden had an example. "In elementary school we read the book, *A Single Shard* by Linda Sue Park, and one of the themes in that novel is that learning things the hard way is often the best way. For one example, Tree Ear, the main character, begins with the (5)________________________ that he can easily push a wheelbarrow full of heavy rocks if he arranges the rocks in a balanced way. He only arrives at this idea after the wheelbarrow with rocks placed in a random way tips over as he is trying to push it."

"Perfect example, Aiden. Anyone else?"

"I just watched the *Beauty and the Beast* movie for about the 20th time," said Suzanne. "I think the main theme is that one must look beyond the surface and find what's on the inside. Beauty discovers that beneath Beast's monster-like exterior is a gentle man with a kind and loving (6)___________________________."

"Another example," offered Brendan, "involves the character of Marty from the novel, *Shiloh* that I think we read in the 4th grade. While Marty's action was not a serious a crime such as (7)___________________________, Marty did steal the dog Shiloh from Judd Travers. The reason he kept Shiloh away from Judd is that Judd abused his dogs and sometimes even killed them. So one theme of that novel might be that a person's view of what's right and wrong sometimes changes when he or she becomes emotionally involved in a problem. Marty loved Shiloh and couldn't stand to see the dog abused."

"Excellent example, Brendan," complimented Mrs. Cole.

Gary raised his hand and said his theme was from *The Three Little Pigs*, and everyone laughed. "Haste makes waste, and it's better to take your time and do something right is definitely a theme," said Gary. "The big bad wolf couldn't blow the third little pig's home down, because he worked hard and built his home with bricks, while the other two took the lazy way of building with straw and sticks."

 

"I think that even a political cartoon can have a theme," said Max. In a magazine were (8)__________________________ of a dad working at his computer with his kid standing next to him saying, 'In return for an increase in my allowance, I can offer you free unlimited in-home computer tech support.' I think the cartoonist's theme is that kids are often more computer literate than adults."

"Good point, Max. Also, Aesop's fables have morals, which are similar to themes. The theme of one fable is about the dangers of (9)__________________________. In the fable, 'The Scorpion and the Frog,' the frog says that he will give the scorpion a ride across the pond on his back if the scorpion will swear not to sting him. But alas, the scorpion cannot resist and stings the frog, and they both drown. One theme might be that when you lie, you not only hurt someone else, but you can also hurt yourself," explained Mrs. Cole.

"Be attentive to theme when you read," reminded Mrs. Cole as class ended for the day.

Naturalist Novelists

- Theodore Dreiser
- Thomas Hardy
- Stephen Crane
- John Steinbeck
- Kate Chopin
- Jack London

 

**D.** The underlined part in each sentence is a synonym, idiom, phrase, or definition for a list word. Unscramble the list word and write the word on the blank.

1. Everyone laughed when Ned put his hand on his forehead and said, "I have a strong feeling that Emmalin will say, 'Yes,' when I ask her to go to the dance." ____________ niponritemo

2. "I appreciate your honesty," said Principal Zhang after questioning a group of students concerning their feelings about school rules. ____________ darcno

3. Mrs. Denby's good-humored, genial personality makes music class fun. ____________ amepetrtnem

4. Ms. Steinman had her art students sketch a comic representation of one of their teachers. ____________ atiucercar

5. In writing class, John began his science fiction story with the theory that life could exist in another galaxy. ____________ sepierm

6. The high erratic winds caused disorder and high waves in the sea. ____________ utbenrulec

7. Speaking on lying, Friedrich Nietzsche once said, "I'm not upset that you lied to me. I'm upset that from now on I can't believe you." ____________ edietc

8. The songs of Bob Dylan reflected the conflict of the 1960s. ____________ beluetcrun

9. The most famous case of art theft occurred in 1911, when the Mona Lisa was stolen from the Louvre, but it was recovered two years later. ____________ neylcra

10. Hope's mother finds peacefulness in her busy life when she practices yoga. ____________ ntersyei

**E.** Write the word, idiom, or phrase from the choice box that best defines each list word.

- foreboding
- chaos in nature
- burglary
- disposition
- confusion
- sincerity
- stillness
- parody
- hypothesis
- guile
- ancestry

1. serenity ____________________
2. larceny ____________________
3. turbulence ____________________
4. temperament ____________________
5. deceit ____________________
6. turbulence ____________________
7. premonition ____________________
8. caricature ____________________
9. premise ____________________
10. candor ____________________

**F.** Complete each sentence to show that you understand the meaning of the underlined word.

1. A premonition that would make Hannah smile is ________________________________
________________________________________________________________.

2. A caricature of ______________ would show the following features exaggerated: ____
________________________________________________________________.

3. A place where Mrs. Denby finds serenity is ____________________________________
________________________________________________________________.

4. Luke discovered that a consequence of deceit is ______________________________
________________________________________________________________.

5. Mr. Clark explained that one cause of turbulence among the people of a nation might be
________________________________________________________________.

6. Mrs. Bradley said that a premise that might lead to an interesting science experiment would be ________________________________________________________
________________________________________________________________.

7. Rachel's candor was appreciated when _________________________________________
________________________________________________________________.

8. A time when Max experienced turbulence in nature was ________________________
________________________________________________________________.

9. If Tim was asked to describe the temperament of his friend he would say ___________
________________________________________________________________.

10. As the victim of larceny, Shane was seriously upset because ___________________
________________________________________________________________.

# Vocabulary List 20
## All-Important Adjectives

| **Word**<br>[pronunciation]<br>**other word form** | **Definition**<br>• sample sentence |
|---|---|
|  |  |
| **amenable**<br>[uh MEE nuh buhl]<br>**amenability** (n) | ready or willing to answer, act, agree, or yield<br>• Celeste was amenable to letting Cindy choose the movie they would see. |
| **congenial**<br>[kuhn JEEN yuhl]<br>**congeniality** (n) | agreeable, pleasant, and friendly in nature or character<br>• Because Emmalin was so congenial, she had many friends. |
| **counterfeit**<br>[KOUN ter fit]<br>**counterfeiter** (n) | an imitation passed off as genuine in an attempt to defraud<br>• Counterfeit $100 bills do not have a watermark that appears when backlit. |
| **definitive**<br>[dih FIN ih tiv] | reliable, complete, and not subject to change<br>• May 12 was the definitive date for the field trip to the Planetarium. |
| **diffident**<br>[DIF ih duhnt]<br>**diffidence** (n) | lacking confidence in one's own ability, worth, or fitness<br>• Celeste was diffident with strangers, but outgoing with her friends. |
| **superfluous**<br>[soo PUR floo uhs]<br>**superfluousness** (n) | exceeding what is necessary or required<br>• Henry David Thoreau's *Walden* focused on living simply instead of accumulating superfluous material things. |
| **transcendent**<br>[tran SEN duhnt]<br>**transcendence** (n) | beyond the limits of ordinary experience<br>• David Copperfield is a transcendent magician who makes the impossible look easy. |
| **urbane**<br>[ur BEYN]<br>**urbanity** (n) | polite and polished in manner<br>• Mr. Stewart, a world traveler, was urbane and poised in any setting. |
| **voracious**<br>[vaw REY shuhs] | having a huge appetite or a great eagerness for something<br>• Aiden had a voracious appetite for learning about history. |

**A.** Write the best list word that the synonyms, idioms, or phrases define to complete each sentence.

| | | | |
|---|---|---|---|
| quixotic | counterfeit | transcendent | voracious |
| amenable | diffident | urbane | congenial |
| definitive | superfluous | | |

1. The ___________________________ atmosphere of the school made new students feel welcome.
   hospitable pleasant sociable convivial

2. Because of her fear of heights, Heidi's friends were surprised when she said she was ___________________________ to try bungee-jumping.
   cooperative acquiescent compliant willing

3. ___________________________ art dates back to ancient times when Roman sculptors produced copies of Greek sculptures.
   forged fake bogus phony

4. Gary's grandparents, who lived in rural Iowa, enjoyed the ___________________________ setting of New York City where they enjoyed attending concerts and visiting museums.
   suave sophisticated cultured cosmopolitan

5. After their soccer game, the girls had a/an ___________________________ appetite so the coach took them to In-N-Out Burger.
   ravenous insatiable gluttonous hungry

6. "Ursula LeGuin's novels, such as *The Earthsea Trilogy* are___________________________," claimed Julia. "They take the reader to another world."
   incomparable unparalleled mystical unique

7. "___________________________ items must be left behind when packing a backpack for a long hike; only essential items can be taken," reminded the trail guide.
   nonessential redundant uncalled for extra

8. The Warren Commission Report that investigated the assassination of JFK was ___________________________ in stating that a lone gunman took Kennedy's life.
   final conclusive absolute accepted

9. Everyone was surprised when the usually ___________________________ Max said he wanted to be a stand-up comedian some day.
   bashful timid insecure self-conscious

 

**B.** Write the best word from the choice box to complete each sentence.

| | | | |
|---|---|---|---|
| amenability | nefarious | definitive | diffidence |
| superfluousness | voracious | congeniality | counterfeiter |
| transcendence | urbanity | | |

1. Mandy has such a ________________________ appetite for learning new vocabulary words that she installed five dictionaries on her laptop computer.

2. With __________________________, Bernie agreed to let Aiden choose the movie they would see.

3. "I thought you might do fairly well on the geography test," said Mr. Clark, "but for all of you to get A's and B's gives me a feeling of proud _________________________ of my expectations."

4. "Brendan, you have a look of __________________________ with your white shirt and tie and carrying your briefcase," complimented Ms. Palmer on the day of class debates.

5. "Consider the deadline for science research papers as __________________________ ," advised Mrs. Bradley. "I will not extend the deadline, nor will I accept late papers without a very good reason."

6. Principal Zhang asked Matt—a student known for his __________________________—to help greet parents on orientation day for prospective students.

7. The ___________________________ forged a painting by Jan van Eyck and tried to pass it off as genuine and sell it to a wealthy art collector.

8. When Caroline held a dog biscuit in her hand, she was able to overcome the ____________________________ of the hungry, stray dog as it came slowly to her.

9. "____________________________ in word usage does not impress me," reminded Ms. Paterson. "It is more important to be concise and thoughtful as you support your thesis."

## C. Story Challenge

Write the best word from the choice box to fill each blank in the story.

| | | | |
|---|---|---|---|
| amenable | congenial | superfluous | urbane |
| condescending | definitive | transcendent | voracious |
| perpetual | diffident | | |

### How Are You Feeling?

When Mr. Riley's writing students were seated he began, "'In the movie *Forest Gump*, Forest muses about how his mother always compared life to a box of chocolates. Can anyone explain the comparison between life and a box of chocolates?" he asked.

John was familiar with the movie, so he said, "In life, you never know what you're going to get, just like in a box of chocolates; sometimes you have to bite into a chocolate to see what's in the center."

"Good John," said Mr. Riley. "Our focus will be on similes and your assignment will be to write a poem using a series of similes that describe a mood or a feeling. For example, a student I had in the past wrote the following poem titled, "I'm Feeling Apprehensive." What does the word apprehensive mean?" he asked.

"The word means nervous about something coming in the future or is about to happen," said Kara.

"Good, Kara. As I read Annie's poem, notice that her title states the feeling she is about to describe and her similes explain her apprehensive feelings.

**I'm Feeling Apprehensive**

like a gazelle imagining a lion hiding in the brush
like biting into an oyster for the first time
like opening an envelope with a return address of a person I don't know
like a cat seeing a German shepherd approach
like walking close to the edge of the Grand Canyon

like wondering if he will notice me

"I like that poem," said Cindy. "Annie skips a line and then tells us the real reason for her apprehension. With her similes, the reader can imagine how she feels."

"Let's have some fun with the vocabulary words," said Mr. Riley. Because they are all adjectives, let's add a simile line to each of the words."

 

Shane volunteered to be first. "I feel (1) ________________________________," he began, "like a politician shaking hands with potential voters."

Julia was next. "My decision is (2) ________________________________," she said, "like knowing if I don't get enough sleep, I'll be crabby."

Dylan was next. "I'm (3) ________________________________," he declared, "like vultures in the jungle rushing to a fresh kill."

Heidi had her hand raised. "I'm (4) ________________________________," she said, "like wanting to hide under the desk."

"Bernie?" Mr. Riley asked. "His smile is (5) ________________________________," Bernie said, "like a fake $100 bill."

Hope raised her hand to be next. "My dreams are (6) ________________________________ she said, "like flying above the clouds with wings of gold ."

Mr. Riley called on Brendan next. "My friend is (7) ________________________________ he said, "like a top hat, bow tie, and tuxedo."

"I have an example," said Aiden. "My little brother is (8) ____________________________, like a rubber man that can bend any which way."

"From your examples, I look forward to your poems," said Mr. Riley. "No need to be (9) ____________________________. Quality is more important than quantity. Compose your poem with at least six good similes to illustrate the mood you choose. Then, like Annie does, skip a line after your similes and add the real reason for your feelings. First decide on your mood; joyful, serious, sad, bored, strong, shy, confident, worried, embarrassed, or confused might be some choices. After you've decided your mood, brainstorm your similes and then compose your poem."

"I'm nervous about my history test next period," said Max on the way out of class. "Maybe I'll use 'nervous' for my simile-mood poem."

### Similes & Metaphors

- A simile is a comparison using like or as.
  His heart is like stone.
- A metaphor is a comparison that does not use like or as.
  He has a heart of stone.

**D.** The underlined part in each sentence is a synonym, idiom, phrase, or definition for a list word. Unscramble the list word and write the word on the blank.

1. Wearing a raincoat, a rain hat, and carrying an umbrella may be more than what is needed. ____________ oefusulpsur

2. A final conclusion in the world of science is often risky because of new discoveries. ____________ nietfidevi

3. Ms. Steinman explained that the artistic visions of Surrealist artists such as Rene Magritte and Salvador Dali are often beyond ordinary experience. ____________ snatnetrencd

4. The street vendor was trying to sell imitation Louis Vuitton bags as though they were authentic. ____________ retfcteioun

5. Many citizens were not agreeable to new taxes and protested loudly. ____________ lenaebma

6. "I don't have a huge appetite except when it comes to spaghetti and meatballs," explained Casey as he asked for a third helping. ____________ ariuvosoc

7. John's mother complimented Shane on his polite and friendly behavior when he came to their house for dinner. ____________ nuebra

8. Working in groups in social studies class helped Julia to be more talkative and less timid. ____________ ftiednfid

9. Many students liked to discuss problems with Ann, because she was a non-judgmental, friendly listener. ____________ nelonciga

**E.** Write the word, idiom, or phrase from the choice box that best defines each list word.

- extra
- good-natured
- sophisticated
- ravenous
- agreeable
- bashful
- decisive
- fake
- unmatched
- unrealistic

1. definitive ______________________________
2. urbane ______________________________
3. transcendent ______________________________
4. amenable ______________________________
5. superfluous ______________________________
6. diffident ______________________________
7. voracious ______________________________
8. congenial ______________________________
9. counterfeit ______________________________

**F.** Complete each sentence to show that you understand the meaning of the underlined word.

1. Three things that might be counterfeited are ______________________________
______________________________________________________________.

2. The most urbane person I know is ____________________ because ______________
______________________________________________________________.

3. Ms. Cosgrove, the gym teacher is definitive about ____________________________
______________________________________________________________.

4. A movie or book that might be described as transcendent is ______________________
because _______________________________________________________.

5. It was obvious that Bella is a diffident person because __________________________
______________________________________________________________.

6. It might be a positive thing to have a superfluous amount of ______________________
because _______________________________________________________.

7. One can recognize Matthew as a congenial person by ____________________________
______________________________________________________________.

8. Cindy has a voracious interest in ______________________________ and enjoys
______________________________________________________________.

9. The students in Ms. Paterson's writing class were amenable to the idea of ____________
______________________________________________________________.

# Review: Lists 17-20

**A.** Use the clues to complete the crossword puzzle with vocabulary words, synonyms, or information from the activities.

**Across**

4. Actions or words that incite
5. A petulant person might do this
7. To give up something
10. Superfluous
12. Temperament
15. Coalesce
16. Palatable
18. Genuine

**Down**

1. Disappear
2. Wicked
3. A premonition
6. Turbulence
8. Unrealistic
9. Deceit
11. Caricature
13. A dilatory person might be...
14. Repudiate
17. Something perpetual has no...

**B.** Circle the answer which best completes the sentence.

1. She is **amenable** because she
   a. eats too much junk food.
   b. is cooperative.
   c. gets good grades

2. An **urbane** person might
   a. raise hogs.
   b. slurp his soup.
   c. buy tickets to the symphony.

3. To find **serenity** she
   a. went to a rock concert.
   b. took a walk in the park.
   c. joined her family for dinner.

4. One guilty of grand **larceny** may have
   a. robbed a bank.
   b. lied under oath.
   c. forged a passport.

5. Someone with **candor** is
   a. intelligent.
   b. truthful.
   c. lazy.

6. A **voracious** person is
   a. hungry.
   b. nonchalant.
   c. tired.

7. A **didactic** presentation would
   a. entertain.
   b. instruct.
   c. amuse.

8. A person **debilitated** would be
   a. invigorated.
   b. anxious.
   c. weakened.

9. One who **vacillates** might be described as
   a. eager.
   b. intelligent.
   c. indecisive

10. A **premise** could be compared to a
    a. proposition.
    b. prioritized list.
    c. novel.

**C.** From the list of fictional book titles, write the best word that might be used in each book.

| | | |
|---|---|---|
| absolve | definitive | curtail |
| congenial | counterfeit | incendiary |
| parsimonious | transcendent | diffident |
| espouse | turbulence | |

1. ______________________ *Guide to Spiritual Meditation*

2. ______________________ *Overcoming Shyness and Uncertainty*

3. ______________________ *The Firefighter's Handbook*

4. ______________________ *Stop Spending and Start Saving*

5. ______________________ *The Ultimate Blueprint for a Happy Life*

6. ______________________ *Storms at Sea: A Sailor's Story*

7. ______________________ *The Power of Forgiveness*

8. ______________________ *Champion for Equality: A Diary of Susan B. Anthony*

9. ______________________ *Xenia: The Importance of Hospitality Embedded in Ancient Greek Culture*

10. ______________________ *Art Forgeries of the 20th Century*

# Answers

**List 1**

**A.** Page 2
1. visceral
2. surreptitious
3. effervescent
4. perspicacious
5. spurious
6. parsimonious
7. tantamount
8. mawkish
9. truculent

**B.** Page 3
1. parsimony
2. surreptitious
3. tantamount
4. spurious
5. effervescence
6. visceral
7. perspicacious
8. mawkish
9. truculence

**C.** Pages 4-5
1. visceral
2. mawkish
3. perspicacious
4. tantamount
5. truculent
6. spurious
7. surreptitious
8. parsimonious
9. effervescent

**D.** Page 6
1. visceral
2. truculent
3. effervescent
4. mawkish
5. spurious
6. perspicacious
7. surreptitious
8. tantamount
9. parsimonious

**E.** Page 7
1. penny-pitching
2. bubbly
3. insightful
4. fake
5. sneaky
6. bad-tempered
7. ingrained
8. maudlin
9. equal to

**F.** Page 8
Sentences will vary.

**List 2**

**A.** Page 10
1. inquisitively
2. solemnly
3. reluctantly
4. inconspicuously
5. judiciously
6. unethically
7. obnoxiously
8. ingeniously
9. impertinently

**B.** Page 11
1. ingenuity
2. inconspicuously
3. solemnity
4. reluctance
5. impertinence
6. judiciously
7. obnoxiously
8. unethically
9. inquisitively

**C.** Pages 12-14
1. reluctantly
2. inquisitively
3. inconspicuously
4. obnoxiously
5. impertinently
6. solemnly
7. unethically
8. judiciously
9. ingeniously

**D.** Page 15
1. unethically
2. inconspicuously
3. reluctantly
4. obnoxiously
5. judiciously
6. solemnly
7. impertinently
8. inquisitively
9. ingeniously

**E.** Page 16
1. hesitantly
2. creatively
3. disrespectfully
4. dignified
5. unnoticeably
6. unpleasantly
7. curiously
8. wisely
9. immorally

**F.** Page 17
Sentences will vary.

**List 3**

**A.** Pages 19-20
1. malign
2. defer
3. accosted
4. acknowledged
5. compensated
6. justified
7. decimated
8. obfuscating
9. compensate
10. litigate
11. acknowledged

**B.** Page 21
1. decimation
2. acknowledgement
3. compensation
4. malign
5. obfuscation
6. litigation
7. justification
8. accosted
9. defer

**C.** Pages 22-24
1. acknowledged
2. obfuscate
3. accosted
4. justify
5. decimated
6. defer
7. litigating

8. acknowledged
9. malign
10. compensate
11. compensated

**D.** Page 25
1. compensated
2. acknowledged
3. deferred
4. litigate
5. obfuscated
6. acknowledged
7. compensated
8. decimated
9. justified
10. malign
11. accosted

**E.** Page 26
1. to thank/to admit existence of
2. exterminate
3. postpone
4. slander
5. to admit existence of/to thank
6. prosecute
7. reimburse/make amends for
8. vindicate
9. waylay
10. make amends for/ reimburse
11. obscure

**F.** Page 27
Sentences will vary.

### List 4

**A.** Page 29
1. homogeneous
2. frugal
3. obsequious
4. grandiose
5. immutable
6. heterogeneous
7. copious
8. ebullient
9. culinary

**B.** Page 30
1. grandiosity
2. culinary
3. frugality
4. ebullience
5. obsequious
6. heterogeneous
7. immutability
8. copious
9. homogeneous

**C.** Pages 31-32
1. ebullient
2. obsequious
3. copious
4. frugal
5. grandiose
6. culinary
7. heterogeneous
8. homogeneous
9. immutable

**D.** Page 33
1. frugal
2. homogeneous
3. obsequious
4. grandiose
5. ebullient
6. copious
7. heterogeneous
8. culinary
9. immutable

**E.** Page 34
1. disparate
2. bombastic
3. fawning
4. savory
5. equal
6. effervescent
7. perpetual
8. stingy
9. plentiful

**F.** Page 35
Sentences will vary.

### Review: Lists 1-4

**A.** Page 36

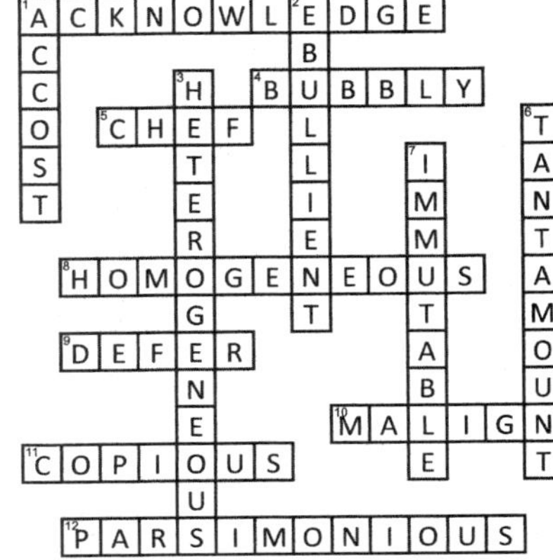


**B.** Page 37
1. b
2. a
3. a
4. b
5. a
6. c
7. c
8. b
9. c
10. a
11. b
12. b

**C.** Page 38
1. mawkish
2. inquisitively
3. unethically
4. ingeniously
5. truculent
6. inconspicuously
7. visceral
8. justify
9. obfuscate
10. spurious
11. acknowledge
12. surreptitious

### List 5

**A.** Page 40
1. Incorrect
2. Incorrect
3. Correct
4. Correct
5. Incorrect
6. Correct
7. Correct

8. Incorrect
9. Incorrect

**B.** Pages 41-42
1. disconcerting
2. egalitarianism
3. nebulous
4. autodidact
5. infallibility
6. clandestine
7. peripatetic
8. stoicism
9. banality

**C.** Pages 43-44
1. disconcerting
2. nebulous
3. banal
4. clandestine
5. autodidactic
6. peripatetic
7. stoic
8. egalitarian
9. infallible

**D.** Page 45
1. egalitarian
2. peripatetic
3. clandestine
4. disconcerting
5. infallible
6. autodidactic
7. banal
8. stoic
9. nebulous

**E.** Page 46
1. unemotional
2. hush-hush
3. frequent traveler
4. equitable
5. obscure
6. disturbing
7. commonplace
8. self-taught
9. flawless

**F.** Page 54
Sentences will vary.

**List 6**

**A.** Page 49
1. certitude
2. betrothal
3. demagogue
4. conduit
5. mandate
6. hiatus
7. bravado
8. conduit
9. pandemic
10. ichthyology

**B.** Page 50
1. pandemic
2. ichthyology
3. certitude
4. conduits
5. demagoguery
6. conduit
7. hiatus
8. betrothal
9. mandate
10. bravado

**C.** Pages 51-52
1. bravado
2. betrothal
3. conduit
4. ichthyology
5. pandemic
6. certitude
7. conduit
8. hiatus
9. demagogue
10. mandate

**D.** Page 53
1. conduits
2. demagogue
3. certitude
4. hiatus
5. mandate
6. bravado
7. pandemic
8. ichthyology
9. betrothal
10. conduit

**E.** Page 54
1. channel for fluid or wires/ means of communication
2. certainty
3. official approval
4. widespread disease
5. unethical leader
6. boastfulness
7. means of communication/ channel for fluid or wires
8. study of fish
9. marriage agreement
10. pause in activity

**F.** Page 55
Sentences will vary.

**List 7**

**A.** Page 57
1. Incorrect
2. Incorrect
3. Incorrect
4. Correct
5. Incorrect
6. Correct
7. Correct
8. Incorrect
9. Correct

**B.** Page 58
1. radical
2. facetious
3. decadence
4. obstinance
5. garrulous
6. maritime
7. languid
8. slander
9. lucidity

**C.** Pages 59-61
1. garrulous
2. facetious
3. slanderous
4. radical
5. languid
6. lucid
7. decadent
8. obstinate
9. maritime

**D.** Page 62
1. facetious
2. decadent
3. languid
4. maritime
5. obstinate
6. radical

7. garrulous
8. slanderous
9. lucid

**E.** Page 63
1. defamatory
2. self-indulgent
3. tongue-in-cheek
4. inflexible
5. evident
6. listless
7. nautical
8. loquacious
9. extreme

**F.** Page 64
Sentences will vary.

## List 8

**A.** Page 66
1. antonyms
2. synonyms
3. antonyms
4. antonyms
5. synonyms
6. antonyms
7. synonyms
8. antonyms
9. synonyms

**B.** Page 67
1. conscientiously
2. chivalry
3. coherence
4. clairvoyant
5. curmudgeon
6. chauvinist
7. complaisantly
8. circuitous
9. cynicism
10. chauvinism
11. clairvoyance
12. cynic

**C.** Pages 68-70
1. cynically
2. chivalrously
3. coherently
4. curmudgeonly
5. conscientiously
6. complaisantly
7. clairvoyantly
8. circuitously
9. chauvinistically

**D.** Page 71
1. clairvoyantly
2. chivalrously
3. conscientiously
4. curmudgeonly
5. chauvinistically
6. cynically
7. complaisantly
8. coherently
9. circuitously

**E.** Page 72
1. good-naturedly
2. gallantly
3. psychically
4. prejudicially
5. carefully
6. gruffly
7. rambling
8. clearly
9. distrustfully

**F.** Page 73
Sentences will vary.

## Review: Lists 5-8

**A.** Page 74

| | | | | | | | | | | | | | | |
|---|---|---|---|---|---|---|---|---|---|---|---|---|---|---|
| 1 D | | | | | | | | | 2 P | | | | | |
| 3 I | N | 4 F | A | L | L | I | B | L | E | | | | | |
| S | | I | | | | | | | R | | | | | |
| 5 P | A | N | D | E | M | I | C | | I | | 6 C | | | 7 O |
| A | | S | | | | | | | P | | E | | | B |
| R | | | | | 8 C | H | I | V | A | L | R | O | U | S |
| A | | | | | O | | | | T | | T | | | T |
| G | | | 9 M | A | N | D | A | T | E | | A | | | I |
| I | | | A | | D | | | | T | | I | | | N |
| N | | | R | | U | | | | I | | N | | | A |
| G | | | R | | I | | | | C | | | | | T |
| | | 10 H | I | A | T | U | S | | | 11 T | R | I | 12 T | E |
| | | | A | | | | | | | | | | A | |
| 13 L | A | N | G | U | I | D | | | | | 14 B | O | L | D |
| | | | E | | | | | | | | | | K | |

**B.** Page 75
1. c
2. b
3. b
4. c
5. c
6. b
7. c
8. a
9. b
10. c

**C.** Page 76
1. cynically
2. clandestine
3. autodidactic
4. disconcerting
5. conscientiously
6. complaisantly
7. circuitously
8. lucid
9. radical
10. coherently

## List 9

**A.** Page 78
1. obliterate
2. corroborate
3. confer
4. gesticulate
5. embody
6. fabricate
7. deflect
8. alienate
9. galvanize
10. embody
11. confer

**B.** Page 79
1. alienation
2. conference
3. gesticulations
4. embodiment
5. fabrication
6. galvanization
7. obliterated
8. deflect
9. corroborate

**C.** Pages 80-82
1. corroborated
2. embodies
3. deflect
4. gesticulated
5. confer
6. fabricating
7. obliterate
8. galvanize
9. conferred
10. embody
11. alienate

**D.** Page 83
1. obliterating
2. gesticulated
3. corroborated
4. galvanized
5. deflect
6. conferred
7. embodied
8. conferred
9. alienated
10. fabricated
11. embodied

**E.** Page 84
1. represent/integrate
2. award to/consult
3. divert
4. integrate/represent
5. motion (v)
6. turn away
7. consult/award to
8. destroy
9. validate
10. falsify
11. inspire

**F.** Page 85
Sentences will vary.

**List 10**

**A.** Page 87
1. unctuous
2. condescending
3. gratuitous
4. prehensile
5. unanimous
6. culpable
7. arbitrary
8. retrospective
9. incisive
10. gratuitous

**B.** Page 88
1. retrospection
2. culpability
3. prehensility
4. unanimity
5. arbitrariness
6. condescension
7. incisiveness
8. gratuity
9. incision
10. unctuous

**C.** Pages 89-91
1. unctuous
2. gratuitous
3. culpable
4. condescending
5. retrospective
6. incisive
7. unanimous
8. prehensile
9. arbitrary
10. gratuitous

**D.** Page 92
1. arbitrary
2. gratuitous
3. culpable
4. incisive
5. prehensile
6. unanimous
7. unctuous
8. condescending
9. gratuitous
10. retrospective

**E.** Page 93
1. reminiscent
2. all in accord
3. free/unnecessary
4. superiority
5. able to grasp
6. blameworthy
7. insincere/flattery
8. sharp
9. unnecessary/free
10. unpredictable

**F.** Page 94
Sentences will vary.

**List 11**

**A.** Page 96
1. obscurity
2. idiosyncrasy
3. genealogy
4. quandary
5. obsolescence
6. gastronomy
7. treason
8. manifesto
9. pathos

**B.** Page 97
1. treasonous
2. quandary
3. obsolete
4. obscure
5. pathos
6. genealogy
7. manifesto
8. idiosyncratic
9. gastronomical

**C.** Pages 98-99
1. quandary
2. obscurity
3. manifesto
4. obsolescence
5. genealogy
6. treason
7. idiosyncrasy
8. pathos
9. gastronomy

**D.** Page 100
1. obsolescence
2. pathos
3. quandary
4. idiosyncrasy
5. treason
6. manifesto
7. gastronomy
8. genealogy
9. obscurity

**E.** Page 101
1. proclamation
2. emotion
3. oblivion
4. predicament
5. thing of the past
6. sedition
7. eccentricity
8. ancestry
9. culinary science

F. Page 102
Sentences will vary.

**List 12**

**A.** Pages 104-105
1. objective
2. palpable
3. inchoate
4. quiescent

5. iconic
6. cognizant
7. ludicrous
8. humane
9. omniscient
10. objective

**B.** Page 106
1. cognizant
2. inchoate
3. iconic
4. ludicrous
5. omniscient
6. quiescent
7. objective
8. palpable
9. objective
10. humane

**C.** Pages 107-108
1. omniscient
2. objective
3. cognizant
4. quiescent
5. inchoate
6. iconic
7. palpable
8. ludicrous
9. humane
10. objective

**D.** Page 109
1. ludicrous
2. objective
3. palpable
4. cognizant
5. omniscient
6. quiescent
7. objective
8. humane
9. iconic
10. inchoate

**E.** Page 110
1. prototypical
2. inert
3. embryonic
4. perceptive
5. goal/nonpartisan
6. evident
7. sympathetic
8. absurd
9. all-knowing
10. nonpartisan/goal

**F.** Page 111
Sentences will vary.

**Review: Lists 9-12**

**A.** Page 112

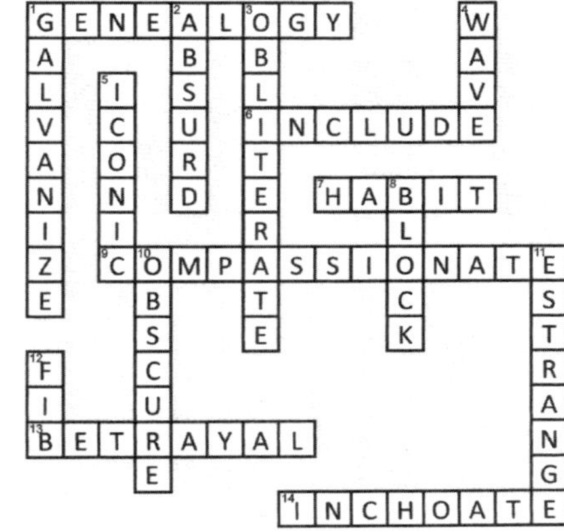


**B.** Page 113
1. b
2. c
3. a
4. b
5. c
6. a
7. a
8. a
9. c
10. c
11. b
12. c
13. c
14. a

**C.** Page 114
1. cognizant
2. prehensile
3. gratuitous
4. confer
5. corroborate
6. manifesto
7. obsolescence
8. quiescent
9. quandary
10. objective
11. arbitrary

**List 13**

**A.** Page 116
1. Incorrect
2. Incorrect
3. Incorrect
4. Correct
5. Incorrect
6. Correct
7. Correct
8. Incorrect
9. Incorrect
10. Correct
11. Incorrect

B. Page 117
1. jurisprudence
2. parasitic
3. fait accompli
4. aplomb
5. interlocutor
6. tome
7. coerce
8. peccadillo
9. discordant

**C.** Pages 118-120
1. discord
2. parasite
3. parasite
4. coercion
5. tomes
6. discord
7. fait accompli
8. jurisprudence
9. aplomb
10. peccadillo
11. interlocutor

**D.** Page 121
1. aplomb
2. discord
3. coercion
4. fait accompli
5. peccadillo
6. tome
7. parasite
8. jurisprudence
9. interlocutors
10. discord
11. parasite

**E.** Page 122
1. poise
2. conversationalist
3. forceful persuasion
4. exploits others/dependent organism
5. heavy book

6. small mistake
7. irrevocable
8. lack of harmony/ disagreement
9. science of law
10. disagreement/lack of harmony
11. dependent organism/ exploits others

**F.** Page 123
Sentences will vary.

**List 14**

**A.** Page 125
1. succinct
2. euphonious
3. ambivalent
4. contemptible
5. empathetic
6. caustic
7. verdant
8. dogmatic
9. cursory
10. caustic

**B.** Page 126
1. contempt
2. euphony
3. ambivalence
4. dogma
5. caustic
6. empathy
7. cursory
8. succinct
9. caustic
10. verdant

**C.** Pages 127-129
1. empathetic
2. ambivalent
3. contemptible
4. euphonious
5. caustic
6. dogmatic
7. verdant
8. succinct
9. cursory
10. caustic

**D.** Page 130
1. euphonious
2. verdant
3. dogmatic
4. empathetic
5. succinct
6. caustic
7. contemptible
8. cursory
9. ambivalent
10. caustic

**E.** Page 131
1. compassionate
2. superficially
3. pithy
4. very bad
5. acerbic/sarcastic
6. opinionated
7. green
8. contradictory
9. harmonious
10. sarcastic/acerbic

**F.** Page 132
Sentences will vary.

**List 15**

**A.** Page 134
1. antonyms
2. synonyms
3. synonyms
4. synonyms
5. antonyms
6. synonyms
7. synonyms
8. antonyms
9. antonyms
10. synonyms

**B.** Page 135
1. waived
2. advocated
3. undermine/jeopardize
4. reconciliation
5. jeopardize/undermine
6. extrapolating
7. conformity
8. reciprocated
9. emulated

**C.** Pages 136-137
1. advocated
2. emulate
3. reconciled
4. extrapolated
5. conform
6. waiving
7. undermine
8. reconcile
9. jeopardized
10. reciprocated

**D.** Page 138
1. jeopardized
2. extrapolated
3. advocated
4. waived
5. conform
6. undermine
7. reciprocated
8. reconcile
9. emulates
10. reconciled

**E.** Page 139
1. put at risk
2. threaten
3. estimate
4. do the same in return
5. comply with
6. dispense with
7. recommend
8. patch things up/make the best of
9. model oneself on
10. make the best of/patch things up

**F.** Page 140
Sentences will vary.

**List 16**

**A.** Page 142
1. prioritized
2. amplify
3. posited
4. censure
5. validated
6. instigated
7. alleged
8. divulged
9. epitomizes

**B.** Page 143
1. position
2. allegation
3. amplification
4. priority
5. divulgence

6. epitome
7. instigation
8. validation
9. censured
10. instigator

**C.** Pages 144-146
1. instigate
2. epitomized
3. censured
4. posit/allege
5. allege/posit
6. validate
7. divulging
8. prioritize
9. amplify

**D.** Page 147
1. divulge
2. posited
3. instigate
4. amplifies
5. validating
6. censured
7. alleged
8. epitomizes
9. prioritized

**E.** Page 148
1. categorize
2. exemplify
3. to claim
4. hypothesize
5. increase loudness
6. express strong disapproval
7. disclose
8. verify
9. motivate

**F.** Page 149
Sentences will vary.

**Review: Lists 13-16**

**A.** Page 150

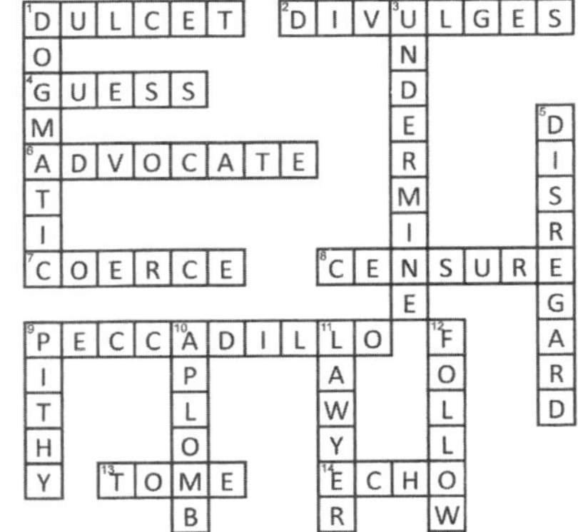

**B.** Page 151
1. a
2. c
3. b
4. c
5. a
6. a
7. b
8. a
9. c
10. b
11. a
12. b
13. c
14. a

**C.** Page 152
1. alleged
2. caustic
3. instigate
4. empathetic
5. fait accompli
6. parasite
7. jeopardize
8. emulate
9. reconcile
10. epitome

**List 17**

**A.** Pages 154-155
1. dilatory
2. incendiary
3. petulant
4. perpetual
5. nefarious
6. quixotic
7. didactic
8. authentic
9. incendiary
10. palatable

**B.** Page 156
1. incendiary
2. quixotic
3. petulance
4. perpetuity
5. authenticity
6. dilatory
7. didactic
8. nefarious
9. palatable
10. incendiary

**C.** Pages 157-158
1. palatable
2. dilatory
3. incendiary
4. didactic
5. authentic
6. quixotic
7. perpetual
8. nefarious
9. petulant

**D.** Page 159
1. nefarious
2. incendiary
3. quixotic
4. incendiary
5. palatable
6. petulant
7. didactic
8. perpetual
9. authentic
10. dilatory

**E.** Page 160
1. evil
2. rousing/combustible
3. tasty
4. forever
5. trustworthy
6. lagging
7. unrealistic
8. combustible/rousing
9. instructive
10. peevish

**F.** Page 161
Sentences will vary.

**List 18**

**A.** Page 163
1. repudiated
2. coalesced
3. vacillated
4. absolve
5. debilitated
6. curtail
7. dissipated
8. espoused
9. relinquish

**B.** Page 164
1. vacillation
2. coalescence
3. espousal
4. absolution
5. debilitation
6. curtailment
7. dissipation
8. repudiation
9. relinquishment

**C.** Pages 165-167
1. vacillated
2. absolve
3. curtailed
4. relinquish
5. espousing
6. debilitated
7. repudiates
8. coalesce
9. dissipate

**D.** Page 168
1. repudiated
2. absolved
3. espoused
4. dissipated
5. relinquish
6. curtailed
7. vacillated
8. debilitated
9. coalesced

**E.** Page 169
1. reject
2. weaken
3. disappear
4. support
5. hesitate
6. unite
7. exonerate
8. give up
9. reduce

**F.** Page 170
Sentences will vary.

**List 19**

**A.** Pages 172-173
1. premonition
2. temperament
3. premise
4. turbulence
5. caricatures
6. deceit
7. candor
8. serenity
9. larceny
10. turbulence

**B.** Page 174
1. temperament
2. larceny
3. deceive
4. serene
5. caricatures
6. turbulent
7. premonitions
8. candid
9. premise
10. deceitful

**C.** Pages 175-177
1. turbulent
2. candor
3. serenity
4. premonition
5. premise
6. temperament
7. larceny
8. caricatures
9. deceit

**D.** Page 178
1. premonition
2. candor
3. temperament
4. caricature
5. premise
6. turbulence
7. deceit
8. turbulence
9. larceny
10. serenity

**E.** Page 179
1. stillness
2. burglary
3. chaos in nature / confusion
4. disposition
5. guile
6. confusion / chaos in nature
7. foreboding
8. parody
9. hypothesis
10. sincerity

**F.** Page 180
Sentences will vary.

**List 20**

**A.** Page 182
1. congenial
2. amenable
3. counterfeit
4. urbane
5. voracious
6. transcendent
7. superfluous
8. definitive
9. diffident

**B.** Page 183
1. voracious
2. amenability
3. transcendence
4. urbanity
5. definitive
6. congeniality
7. counterfeiter
8. diffidence
9. superfluousness

**C.** Pages 184-185
1. congenial
2. definitive
3. voracious
4. diffident
5. counterfeit
6. transcendent
7. urbane
8. amenable
9. superfluous

**D.** Page 186
1. superfluous
2. definitive
3. transcendent
4. counterfeit
5. amenable
6. voracious
7. urbane
8. diffident
9. congenial

**E.** Page 187
1. decisive
2. sophisticated
3. unrealistic
4. agreeable
5. extra
6. bashful
7. ravenous
8. good-natured
9. fake

**F.** Page 188
Sentences will vary.

**Review: Lists 17-20**

**A.** Page 189

| 1 D | | | 2 N | | | | | | | | | 3 H | | |
|---|---|---|---|---|---|---|---|---|---|---|---|---|---|---|
| 4 I | N | C | E | N | D | I | A | R | Y | | 5 S | U | L | K |
| S | | | F | | | | | | | | | N | | |
| S | | | A | | | 6 R | | | | | | C | | |
| I | | | 7 R | E | L | I | N | 8 Q | U | I | S | H | | |
| P | | | I | | | O | | U | | | | | 9 G | |
| A | | | O | | | T | | I | | | | | U | |
| T | | | U | | | | 10 E | X | T | R | A | | I | |
| E | | | S | | | 11 C | | O | | | | | L | |
| | | | | | | 12 A | T | T | I | 13 T | U | D | E | |
| | | | 14 R | | | R | | I | | A | | | | |
| 15 F | U | S | E | | | T | | C | | R | | | | |
| | | | B | | | O | | | 16 E | D | I | B | L | 17 E |
| | | | U | | | O | | | | Y | | | | N |
| | 18 A | U | T | H | E | N | T | I | C | | | | | D |

**B.** Page 190
1. b
2. c
3. b
4. a
5. b
6. a
7. b
8. c
9. c
10. a

**C.** Page 191
1. transcendent
2. diffident
3. incendiary
4. curtail
5. definitive
6. turbulence
7. absolve
8. espouse
9. congenial
10. counterfeit

Sample Activity From
*Critical Thinking Detective™-Vocabulary Book 1*

Read the mystery below to find evidence to identify the innocent and guilty suspects. Remember, the story and suspects' statements are true.

## The Cunning Customer

[1]On December 1 of this year, Jennison City Police investigated the theft of a bracelet from Jennison's Fine Jewelry. [2]The bracelet disappeared between 4 p.m. and 5 p.m. from a display on the jewelry counter. [3]Police interviewed four witnesses. [4]The first witness said the thief was not a devout customer of the store. [5]The second witness said the theft transpired while the sales associate heeded a persnickety customer's tirade. [6]A third witness said the sales associate abetted the thief before she attended to the exacting customer.

[7]Police took the statements from the four suspects listed below. [8]After weighing the evidence, police arrested one of the suspects, who later confessed, and police retrieved the bracelet from her possession later that day.

**Margaret Mathers**

[9]"I was interested in some jewelry but deferred my own questions to the staff until the fastidious customer finished her rant. [10]I saw Helen Speath enter the store amid the harangue."

**Helen Speath**

[11]"The store is not a haunt of mine. [12]I was looking for a gift and came to the store based on the recommendation of a co-worker. [13]I have no convictions about the harried sales associate who left my queries unresolved."

**Anna Knox**

[14]"I am a stalwart fixture in the store and recommended it to my friend, Margaret Mathers. [15]Since then, she has become an inveterate patron."

**Angela Payne**

[16]"I sporadically shop in the store. [17]I found the sales associate to be obliging even though the store was bustling. [18]I can attest to the moiling attention the finicky customer necessitated."

**Based on the evidence, circle the suspect who is the Cunning Customer.**

After solving the case, write the best vocabulary word to complete each sentence. Each word can only be used once.

| | | | | |
|---|---|---|---|---|
| abet | harangue | persnickety | devout | exacting |
| fastidious | query | bustling | inveterate | necessitate |
| obliging | attest | heed | stalwart | transpire |
| amid | harried | sporadically | | |

1. During the summer, the beach is ______________________ with tourists.

2. The ______________________ host provided us with excellent accommodations.

3. The ______________________ fan never misses a basketball game.

4. The collector saw the treasures ______________________ the junk.

5. The impressive trophy ______________________ a custom-built case.

6. Please direct all ______________________ to the information desk.

7. The guide advised the tourists to ______________________ all posted signs.

8. The architect prepared multiple designs for the ______________________ client.

9. ______________________ habits can be difficult to break.

10. Pop-up rain showers happen ______________________ without warning.

11. The loud ______________________ drew stares from bystanders.

12. The clueless substitute unknowingly ______________________ the class troublemaker.

13. After a barrage of questions, the speaker became ______________________.

14. I can ______________________ to the applicant's strong work ethic.

15. The event ______________________ while I was absent.